MODEL MAKING
Technical Skills Using Everyday Objects

MODEL MAKING

Technical Skills Using Everyday Objects

JACK CHARRINGTON PRATT

THE CROWOOD PRESS

First published in 2023 by
The Crowood Press Ltd
Ramsbury, Marlborough
Wiltshire SN8 2HR

enquiries@crowood.com

www.crowood.com

British Library Cataloguing-in-Publication Data
A catalogue record for this book is available from the British Library.

ISBN 978 0 7198 4187 3

Dedication
To my family; proof the hoarding was worthwhile.

Typeset by Simon and Sons
Cover design by Blue Sunflower Creative
Printed and bound in India by Replika Press Pvt Ltd

CONTENTS

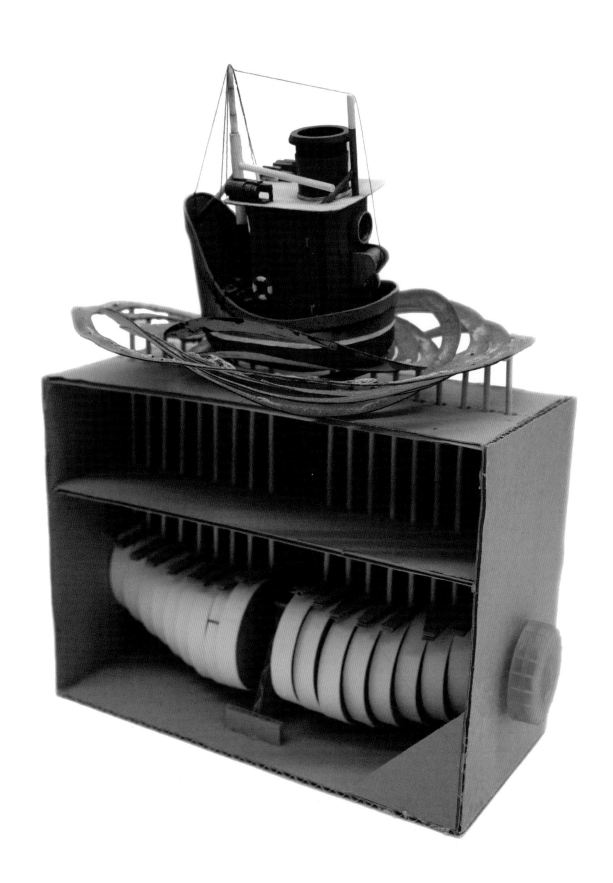

PREFACE

During the summer holidays, I would spend two weeks with my grandparents over in Blackpool. It was on their living room carpet, watching for the umpteenth time the launch sequence of Thunderbird 2, or Stingray weaving around a rather oversized goldfish, that my love of model making was born.

My inspiration has always come from a multitude of sources, not least my father and grandfather, who were both proficient model makers themselves, but it was these works by Gerry Anderson in particular that threw me into a world of fantastical fabrication. I remember hoarding cardboard at every opportunity to recreate these incredible vehicles, and my frustration at my inability to replicate them accurately.

Although I'm sure my family, at the time, would have thought that these cardboard contraptions were simply normal activities for a child to engage in, these early moments in my life would actually form the start of something much bigger. Not only was this my first step into the world of model making, this was also the beginning of my fascination of using found objects and materials to build things beyond even my own imagination.

Today, that journey has transformed into a career. Having studied Set Design for Screen at Wimbledon College of Arts, worked in film and television as a model maker and concept artist, and lectured across various academic institutions, I have been able to develop and refine my skills across a wide range of projects. This work continues both personally and professionally and, while my grandfather is no longer with us to see the outcome of this project, I hope that one day I can sit down with my grandchildren and pass along my experience much the same as he did.

Why I am Writing this Book

In March 2020 I was teaching in London. The students were coming to the end of the academic year and getting ready to start making their final designs. As they were at art college, these designs included miniature model making, props, concept art and full-scale set builds, to name but a few – all of which require substantial resources. In any normal year, sourcing materials would not be an issue. However, at the end of March, the UK entered its first lockdown.

Suddenly, resources were cut off left, right and centre. Academic institutions were ordered to close their doors and all teaching moved online. Understandably, students started to panic, wondering how they could possibly complete their projects without the resources that they had come to depend on.

In fact, we have all become so accustomed to being able to source every single thing we need in our lives at a moment's notice, either from a store or online, that when lockdown came it threw us into a state of shock. From a teacher's perspective, equipment and materials were suddenly restricted, meaning new ways of completing projects had to be found.

As I sat in my tiny flat, I realised that the hobby I had pursued for almost my entire life gave me an opportunity to solve at least one small part of this problem. Students could recognise that they in fact had a wealth of materials that they could access – right in their very homes. They could discover new techniques, new methods of making, without even having to leave the house, and (everybody's favourite) without spending a single penny. Through using these materials, the environment would also benefit, as the students would simultaneously be recycling.

This is why I am writing this book – to open people's minds to the treasure trove of materials that regularly go unappreciated, and to demonstrate some of the many wonderful techniques and processes that anyone of any skill can use to make some truly exceptional creations.

OPPOSITE: **A fishing boat automaton made from found objects and materials. This was constructed during lockdown as an example to students showing how materials around the home could be used to implement their designs to great effect.**

INTRODUCTION

What Material Should I Use for This?

I have heard this question time and time again in the studio. It often comes from panicking students who hold an undying belief that there is a holy model-making doctrine they must follow for anything they might want to make – for example, stating that a cobblestone wall must always be made from styrofoam. To go against this preconception would be to invite chaos into the world and wreak havoc upon their attempt to construct said wall out of any other material.

A little dramatic perhaps, but my time in education has shown that students really can be worryingly reluctant to venture into something blind and rely solely on trial and error to see them through it. By extension, this is also likely to apply to model makers of all backgrounds who may be taking their first steps into the medium and feel equally worried over making any form of mistake.

So, let us begin with the first important point: things will go wrong. This is not meant as a preachy form of encouragement, but as a practical starting point. Making mistakes in model making is how almost all of our knowledge is acquired. It is not necessarily knowing what to do, but what not to do. It bears particular relevance to this book, as many of the methods described in Part II have either been discovered or developed by pure accident, as none of the materials each process requires were actually intended for that purpose.

Which brings us back to the original question and the overarching concept of this book: what material should I use for this? The answer is to ask a different question.

What is the Aim of this Book?

The overall aim of this book is to educate the reader on how to use found objects and materials for model making.

OPPOSITE: **A sci-fi racing vehicle kit bashed from a wide range of found objects. It did not matter what the materials were – what mattered was shape, form, detail and narrative. What did each piece contribute to the build?**

Underpinning this is the need to eradicate the idea that a certain material is required for any one job. Instead, a model maker should ask what qualities does the material need to be effective in a particular situation, and to achieve the desired texture and finish? A model maker should be analytical and objective, and not rely on a job list of materials.

Consequently, this book should form a stepping stone into experimentation, and to begin a better observation of the model maker's environment. Objects and materials should transform themselves into a wealth of potential surfaces and creations.

While there are many practical teaching points in this book, the main hope is that the first question – what should I use for this? – can be replaced with a question that will not only solve the immediate problem, but open so many doors into the world of model making: what can I *do* with this?

How is this Book Arranged?

This book is divided into three sections. Part I, composed of three chapters, will cover all of the introductory information needed to commence a standard miniature project, including construction methods, materials, paints, adhesives and much more.

Part II will explore step-by-step processes that demonstrate how a wide range of textures and surfaces can be created with household materials. This section has been split into four chapters that cover common effects found in model making – scenery, weathering, architecture and interiors.

Part III consists of three projects that bring together everything covered in the previous two sections and offers an opportunity to apply that knowledge to a specific build, again in a step-by-step format.

Why a Scratch-Build Section in a Book for Found Materials?

It may be confusing that, given the emphasis of Part II on the use of found objects and materials, that Part I focuses predominantly on scratch-building techniques; the reason for this is twofold.

Firstly, it is important to grasp the fundamentals of model making before attempting the bigger challenge of using found objects and materials that were never intended for this purpose. These materials have noticeable limitations in their new role and, to use them effectively, it is important to have a good understanding of material properties.

Secondly, many of the materials discussed in Chapter 1 are routinely integrated in kit-bashing projects, just not necessarily in their raw sheet form (more on that later). For example, an understanding of how to work with wood will support the use of common kit-bashing objects such as coffee stirrers and popsicle sticks.

in order to ensure the best possible outcome. In Part II, making literacy is more directly addressed through the analysis of texture, and how crucial it is to identify the real-world qualities of the intended build before actually commencing it.

An academic would no doubt offer a more succinct yet all-encompassing definition, but at the very least this book can offer an introduction to what should be recognised as one of the most fundamental principles of model making. Why we do things, as opposed to how we do things, tends to be what defines the difference between an amateur and a professional – a principle most of us understand but are often completely unaware of!

Making Literacy

Making literacy is all about the reasoning and understanding behind what we make. It is a broad term that a thousand-word essay would struggle to define satisfactorily, but in this book, it is used to explore why a model is being made, its function and purpose. It is used to explain the way a piece of equipment is used as opposed to what it is used for, and even to appreciate the very thing we are trying to make. It is difficult to accurately depict a wave in miniature without an understanding and appreciation for what it is in real life.

In Part I, making literacy takes the form of how to prepare for making a model, and all of the questions that need to be asked

Sustainability

One key reason to adopt found objects and materials into projects is that it is an incredibly sustainable form of making. It is simply another way of recycling and, in today's world, any change to our lives that can be made to benefit the environment is worth consideration. Throughout this book, materials have been chosen for a number of reasons and sustainability is a significant factor. The methods taught in this book may not be 100 per cent sustainable, but I hope that it goes some way to promoting more environmentally friendly methods of making within the model making industry.

PART I: ESSENTIALS AND MODEL-MAKING PRACTICE

CHAPTER 1

CHOOSING YOUR APPROACH

Things to Consider

It is often difficult to know where to begin when first considering model making. The actual physical build is just one element of many that goes into the process of creating a miniature, and when all other aspects are taken into account, the process can suddenly seem quite daunting. For this reason, it is of great importance to consider the best approach and formulate a plan of action before diving straight in.

The term 'approach' in this instance can include a great many things. It does not just refer to the method of making that will be employed, but rather a range of criteria based on the role and purpose of the model. Five important variables to consider in all scenarios are:

- How will the model be used?
- Where will the model be stored?
- What materials will be used?
- Where will materials be sourced from?
- How much time do you have?

These considerations are crucial as they will define everything about the model, and thus form our first encounter with making literacy. These questions will determine whether or not a model needs to be functional, if it needs to be made so that it is easy to repair or replicate, and the one that is almost always forgotten – if it will need cleaning! While this level of detail may seem excessive, even if the model concerned is just an Airfix kit, considering these points before commencing a project can save hours of additional work and ensure that the completed model will be presented in the best possible way. The worst scenario is to be proud of a finished model and then to have it spoiled by complacency.

Purpose

'Purpose' concerns the practical side of the build. Does the model need to function? If so, how will this be achieved? How will mechanics or electrics need to be accounted for in the build? Will the model be touched? If so, what materials will be needed to ensure it withstands brute force, or even the occasional accident?

For the majority of model makers, this point may seem irrelevant, but even hanging a model airplane from the ceiling requires some thought with regards to practicality. How will it be suspended? How will the model be reinforced to withstand its own weight? Can it be easily repaired if it drops? With just these few questions, it is hopefully beginning to become clear how much time and effort thinking about these basic issues can save.

Storage

A crucial point that is so often overlooked, the question of storage can cause immense frustration. Imagine constructing, painting and finishing a superb diorama before realising that there is nowhere safe to put it. Notice the word 'safe' – if a model is going to be on display, it is important to ensure that nothing else can fall onto or knock it. Make sure there is some resistance on the display surface so that it cannot slide easily (living on a boat, I am all too familiar with this). Display cases are fantastic, although often expensive, and just a quick thought on this point will avert cost from a number of angles.

If the model is not going to be on display, ensure it is packaged with care and consideration. This means that it is protected and secure, not wrapped up in several inches of cardboard and tape! Improper wrapping and containers can damage a model more extensively than carelessness, so use soft packing like foam, place supports where the model is strong and leave free space where it is delicate. If the model cannot be seen through the packaging, clearly label it on the outside so the container cannot be mistaken.

Choice of Material

This point is slightly moving ahead, as it assumes that the method of construction has already been decided. Although this comes later, it is important to have in mind the effects that the previous two points will have on the chosen materials. For instance, if a model will be stored somewhere damp, or even exposed to the elements, then porous materials such as wood will not be an ideal choice. Likewise, a model made from styrene will not fare particularly well if exposed to extreme heat. Remember that even moderate environments such as living rooms, over time, will have some form of effect on a model, even if it is just the simple gathering of dust. The choice of materials can make maintenance like dusting much easier and can significantly increase the longevity of a model.

Sourcing Materials

This is especially important to consider if working to a deadline. Ensure that a thorough sweep of the local area has been completed before starting a build so that there is a firm understanding of where materials can be sourced quickly. It is no good, when working to a deadline, to have the one supplier of an essential material two weeks' shipping away. Even for the humble hobbyist, this can be irritating. Another important consideration is overseas shipment. If materials or equipment needs to be sourced abroad, have allowances for shipping and tax been made? Establishing reliable and accessible suppliers can not only save money, but can also help to build a relationship with store owners, who are often sources of incredibly useful knowledge.

Time

Do not think that this applies only to those working to deadlines, for all model makers will at some point fall foul of steadily lengthening lead times. How many projects have been started and ten years later still await completion? This point concerns both the time that will be dedicated towards a build and the setting of a goal to move the project forward when difficult or tedious processes are encountered. Model makers always seem to reach a specific moment in a build that they just wish would end, and it is in these moments that motivation starts to fade away. Setting a time goal, a checklist, or a simple period throughout the day in which to work solidly on a project will help to eliminate several problems – the most important being keeping it off of the 'still to complete' shelf!

ESSENTIAL SUMMARY

- A model can last a lifetime and beyond. Ensure that as much planning goes into what comes after construction as before.
- Gather the resources needed to complete the build before it starts to ensure efficient workflow.
- Create a checklist of tasks to complete – this is not just to improve organisation but to help encourage you through more tedious parts of the project.
- Practise – do not just decide to use a certain material. Try out your selection first to familiarise yourself with its qualities and limitations.

Construction Methods

Once the important organisational details have been finalised, it's time to think about one of the biggest decisions when commencing any project – what construction method will be used? This generally falls into three categories:

- Scratch building
- Kit bashing
- Model kits

The decision over which method to use is generally quite straightforward. It is more often a case of tailoring a method to

A kit-bashed engine prior to priming. Sci-fi and fantastical objects can be given an amazing level of credibility if they reference real world objects. In this instance, I was trying to create a NASA-esque booster.

A small Star Wars diorama. The AT-ST stands atop an ice floe made from filler. The properties of the filler mimic snow beautifully, even down to the odd reflective particle.

a specific skill set than averting future problems, so will tend to come down to simply what is easiest for a particular individual.

Looking solely at ease, beginner modellers will find no better introduction than plastic kits, which can be found anywhere from hobby shops to supermarkets. Familiar brands such as Revell and Airfix provide a wide range of model kits, from aircraft to ships, including more specialised accessory kits for dioramas. These kits vary in difficulty and can be easily assembled with a minimal toolkit. The downside is that one is completely at the mercy of the quality of the kit as it is presented. With increased skill, modellers can use putty, styrene and many other model-making materials to increase the detail and overall quality of the model, which starts to bring in those scratch-building skills that the professional model maker relishes.

Both scratch building and kit bashing represent an increase in difficulty. Both are wonderful methods of making and both present their own unique challenges. Scratch building, the art of making a model predominantly from sheet and raw materials, allows for complete control and endless possibilities. With the right understanding, anything can be constructed. However, this can take years to acquire, and not every model maker will have access to the specific tools and equipment needed to work with certain materials.

Kit bashing, on the other hand, is a method of fabricating using found objects and materials, which eliminates the majority of the processes needed to mould the material itself. It is incredibly cheap, as materials are sourced not from specialist modelling stores but from recycling bins, old circuitry and model kits, to name but a few. A knowledge of adhesives is paramount, and training the eye to foresee what a model will become can be challenging with the kit-bashing method, particularly when the build consists of a jumbled-up mess of a weekend's recycling!

So even just looking at the relative ease of each method opens up a world of possibilities, and may be a little overwhelming. Here is a quick breakdown of the pros and cons of each technique to make the comparison a little easier:

	Pros	Cons
Scratch building	• Absolutely anything can be built; perfect for real-life modelling • Scaling up or down often only involves changing the amount of material used • Expense can be spared by bulk buying certain materials	• Scratch building typically requires greater technical skill • Tools and equipment to work with certain materials may not be immediately accessible • Can arguably increase the time required to complete a project as a result of fabricating everything from scratch
Kit bashing	• Incredibly cheap, as the materials are often sourced from found objects • Sustainable, as it is effectively recycling • Often much quicker than other processes, as forms can be hastily assembled	• Less control over the materials used • Can be difficult to see the end product whilst constructing • A quality paint finish is essential, so those who have less confidence in their painting skills may naturally be put off this method
Model kits	• Easy to assemble, often with step-by-step instructions • Perfect for beginners, as very little skill is initially required • Fun – this is how almost every model maker starts!	• Some instructions can be difficult to follow for a novice • Improving the quality and detail of the model will require more specialist skill • Risk of losing a piece…

Kit Bashing

A thorough understanding of kit bashing is essential to appreciating the underlying essence of this book and will hopefully be the first step into a wonderful exploration of what the process can achieve. The step-by-step guides presented in Part II have their foundations in this technique.

Kit bashing is the art of fabrication using found objects and materials. It is a term that rose in popularity following its masterful use in productions such as *Star Wars* and *Thunderbirds*. Instead of creating a design that was set in stone, forms and details of spaceships and vehicles were built up using readily available objects. In the case of *Star Wars*, it literally was kit bashing, as plastic model kits were torn apart and repurposed to detail the surface of models such as the timeless Star Destroyer.

True kit bashing involves taking pieces from model kits and using their form and detail to build something entirely different. However, kit bashing has evolved into an umbrella term for all things made of 'junk' – a term used lightly and the source of

so many arguments… Included in this term are computer and electronics components, general recycling and a wide variety of miscellaneous materials. The general rule is that the build is constructed from pre-formed objects, no matter if they are complex technological components or a humble bottle cap. Most first forays into kit bashing come in the form of the traditional plastic bottle rocket.

The second key point is that kit bashing involves the combination of any and all materials. There is no one single dominant material, no immediate supply of an identical object, and no amount of control can avoid a build that will naturally evolve of its own accord. Metal is bonded to plastic, plastic to rubber, rubber to sponge and somehow back to metal again. A plastic piece is randomly thrown in but annoyingly, after realising ten more would add a great deal to the overall aesthetic of the build, only one such piece can be found. Subsequently, concessions must be made that ultimately sends the build down an unforeseen avenue. Kit bashing is chaotic and unpredictable, and embracing this fact will unlock its full potential.

A kit-bashed post box. This project was a single-day challenge to use whatever I could find in that day to create a final object that was recognisable.

So how does one take this introductory information and start unlocking said potential? What skills are there even to hone, if any and all materials can be used and planning is somewhat moot as a result of kit bashing's natural and unavoidable evolution? The answer is two words: blending and credibility.

Blending is the make or break of the kit-bashing process. It is very easy to stick a bottle top to a container and call it a jet engine, but it will always stand out as just a bottle top if no further techniques are used. Chosen pieces need to be disguised and blended in to the surface of the model in order to add texture and detail without becoming an eyesore. This can be achieved in various ways, including altering the component by cutting, melting or combining it with others, using weathering effects to add additional texture, or by simply adhering more and more pieces. Be aware, however, that adding too much can cause its own problems.

This is where credibility comes in. Should a piece even be added in the first place? How does one determine what should and shouldn't be added? The answer is credibility. This refers to how believable the build is, and it must always be believable if it is to be effective. Does a piece introduce much-needed texture? Is it square and angular like the rest of the build, or is it curved and more organic-looking? Does it look functional or decorative? Is there anything undesirable that can be easily hidden or removed? All of these questions effect the model's credibility, which can be destroyed by the use of a single wrong piece.

These two concepts embody the skill of kit bashing. It is not quite as easy as raiding the recycling and mashing up whatever comes to hand (although this is a recommended starting point), but with time and dedication this technique can result in creations as imaginative, detailed and inspiring as any made for TV in former times.

ESSENTIAL SUMMARY

- Consider the best approach for the situation and your skill set.
- Scratch building requires great technical skill but with it, anything can be built.
- Kit bashing has limitations but these can be exploited to great effect if control is relinquished.
- Model kits are perfect for the beginner and form most people's entryway into the craft.

CHAPTER 2

TOOLS, EQUIPMENT AND MATERIALS

It is difficult, when walking into a model shop or staring at an endless line of stalls at a trade show, to resist the urge to buy everything and anything in sight. Images of workshops full to the brim with tools and equipment suddenly flash before your eyes, and, before you know it, a basket full of items you barely understand what to do with is in your hands. The simple fact is that a model maker's toolkit takes years to acquire and, in practice, only a handful of items are ever used frequently.

The purpose of this chapter is to identify exactly what those essentials are, including tools, equipment, paints and adhesives. Concentrate on these rather than items that have either one very specific purpose or require skill the novice will not yet have developed.

An Essential Toolkit

Those just starting out in the world of model making do not need to invest hundreds of pounds in fancy tools – these will build up over time (and eventually you may well have doubles and triples of the same item).

- Scalpel
- Steel ruler
- Cutting mat

To the miniature model maker, the scalpel, ruler and mat are the bread and butter of the craft. They will enable the maker to work with a wide range of sheet materials and tackle a good percentage of any project before any more technical piece of equipment is needed. In addition, they are incredibly compact, especially if the modeller opts for an A4-sized cutting mat or smaller, meaning the often large investment in storage can be postponed for a time. These three items will fit happily inside a typical rucksack. Finally, for the prospective student, turning up to work experience or your first job with these three things will ensure that you can contribute to the team right from the off.

Scalpel

A scalpel is typically composed of a metal handle and an interchangeable blade, although many starter sets will have a larger plastic grip to provide better control for the inexperienced. There are many variations, each accompanied by their own blades. The Swann-Morton No. 3 handle is a popular model.

Steel Ruler

A steel rule protects the user when working with a scalpel, as the edge cannot be cut into like a plastic ruler. Safety rulers, which are often shaped like an 'M' or a 'T', offer additional protection against accidental slips of the knife.

Cutting Mat

A cutting mat forms a stable surface on which to use implements such as a scalpel. An important term to look out for is 'self-healing'. This means any cuts made into the mat will seal back up, retaining its smooth surface.

A basic toolkit consisting of a cutting mat, a scalpel and a steel ruler. These three pieces of equipment will form the backbone of the majority of model-making processes.

ESSENTIAL SUMMARY

- A basic toolkit of a scalpel, cutting mat and steel ruler will enable the user to tackle most model-making projects.
- A Swann-Morton scalpel handle opens the user up to a wide selection of blades.
- A safety ruler will offer better protection than a standard steel ruler.
- When looking for cutting mats, consider acquiring several different sizes to assist with both static and mobile workflow.

An Expanded Toolkit

There are simply too many tools and pieces of equipment to include everything in this book, but for the prospective model maker to whom this might seem quite daunting, here is a selection of tools that will prove useful once a steady foothold in the craft has been secured. Again, this list is by no means exhaustive.

Mitre Block

A mitre block enables the user to draw on, cut or saw pieces of material at set angles – most often at 30, 45, 60 and 90 degrees. This eliminates the need to draw and measure angles.

Watch out for the block eventually deteriorating due to damage sustained from tools, in particular saws.

Engineer's Square

An engineer's square's primary function is to enable the user to mark 90-degree angles, but it can also be used to support glued objects, weigh down materials and clamp items together. This is a great multi-purpose tool that improves accuracy of mark making and general construction.

Archimedean Drill

The Archimedean drill is operated by means of a clever little mechanism by which the user slides a grip up and down along a twisted shaft, in turn rotating the drill bit. This often results in more control and a quicker finish than achieved with a pin-vice or other variants.

Hand Saws

Hand saws come in all shapes and sizes and are typically used for cutting wood, although some can be used for other materials such as plastic and foam. Razor saws are the variant most often found in model making, as they are smaller and the blades have much finer teeth than their DIY counterparts.

Files

Files enable the user to smooth rough edges and surfaces. They often need to be used in conjunction with sandpaper, as the teeth on even a needle file (miniature variant) will leave prominent scratches. However, files are a great way to remove large amounts of material quickly, and can be used on a variety of surfaces.

Clamps

Clamps enable the user to hold two objects together, while they focus on another part of the project. The most common, spring clamps, can exert quite a lot of pressure and care should be taken when working with delicate builds. Spreader clamps are a suitable alternative, as they enable the user to determine the amount of pressure exerted.

Scriber

A scriber looks like a scalpel but has a pronounced hooked blade. This blade is perfect for styrene and will remove material forming little spirals of plastic while leaving a perfectly smooth surface. The scribing tool can also be used to remove burrs, soften edges or scribe panel lines into a surface.

Pliers and Cutters

Use a pair of pliers to grab gently and ease a scalpel blade off the handle. Cutters can achieve the same thing, but the edges will be blunted. Cutters are better left for use on removing plastic parts from model kit sprues and for trimming any uneven edges.

Tweezers

If the user is working on a particularly small scale, then tweezers are a must. Reverse tweezers are arguably better suited to the model maker, especially when painting, as pressure is only required to open them. This means the user can work for hours at a time on an incredibly delicate piece without suffering aching limbs or leaving fingerprints on a model.

Sanding Sticks

Sanding sticks are boards or sponges that are backed with abrasive paper. Sanding sticks give the user greater control and last much longer than regular sheets of sandpaper, which tend to crease and disintegrate rather quickly. A sanding block, which usually consists of a solid block of cork, is a good intermediary.

Rotary Tool

The rotary tool is the standout tool in this selection, and potentially the most expensive. A rotary tool is effectively a miniature drill. A large variety of attachments allow the user to drill, saw, sand and perform many of the functions previously mentioned.

A more advanced selection of tools to build up over time. These tools are all exceptionally useful but have more precise applications.

ESSENTIAL SUMMARY

- Many tools are designed for specific purposes and so are used less frequently.
- Acquire tools based upon their relevance to your project – do not purchase them just for the sake of it.
- Manual tools will allow more flexible working – a plug socket is not always easily accessible.
- Tools like a rotary tool that provide many functions that would otherwise require a larger toolset are especially useful.

Although this is an exceptionally useful tool, bear in mind that a power source cannot be guaranteed and, consequently, it should not be taken as a replacement for other, traditional tools. Dremel is a specific brand of rotary tool that has gained particular popularity, but there are other makes available.

Workstations and Storage

The space in which a maker works is just as important as the tools they are working with. It is of vital importance that the maker is sitting comfortably, working at an appropriate height under good lighting and that everything they need is to hand immediately.

There are a number of products that assist with this matter; which product to adopt very much depends upon the individual maker's wants and needs. Hence, again, this list is just a general overview of what to consider and is far from exhaustive.

Workstations

A workstation, in this context, refers to a box that contains everything that one needs to work with. A workstation not only helps to contain mess but, when it comes to tidying away or moving to work in another location, enables the user to simply pack everything away instantly.

While there are a range of products out there, these boxes can be easily custom made and tailored to the maker's individual needs.

'Bits and Bobs' Storage

Organisers come in handy when dealing with all of the tiny bits and pieces that seem to spring up in every build, including loose drill bits, blades and, strangely, used batteries. Really Useful Box is a specific brand whose plastic boxes are quite robust and commonly found on the high street.

Storage bins are a similar system but mounted on walls. These consist of a large metal rack onto which small bins (looking like miniature skips) are hooked in place.

Toolboxes and Organisers

The most obvious companion to any maker: the toolbox. These can range from small plastic lever-arch tubs to huge units composed of individual stackable cases. As this is quite an important purchase for any prospective model maker, especially students who need to transport their equipment regularly between home and studio, it is better not to ask 'which is the best toolbox to buy' but instead to analyse each individual requirement, including:

Lid – Some lids simply hinge back. Others are cantilevered, meaning they pivot and remain level. This is beneficial as storage compartments can be easily accessed.
Space – A big, open toolbox is great for large tools, but dividers help to organise the contents and saves time when packing away.
Trays – Some toolboxes have inner trays that can be lifted out – great for mobility.

Compartments – Individual boxes which can be lifted out are a great way of keeping everything neat and tidy.
Handle – Take into consideration the grip and build quality of the handle.
Mobility – Carrying a heavy toolbox by its handle can be difficult – look for wheels and an extendable handle.
Organisers – Sometimes a small storage unit is all that is required. There are various organisers available that contain useful compartments and dividers similar to toolboxes. One thing to look out for is whether or not the organiser can stack with a toolbox, which is always a great space-saving feature.
Condition – Often lids can be cracked, plastic corners chipped off or compartments missing. Take note of these before purchasing.

One thing that should be mentioned separately is size. The simple fact is that most model makers will fill the space they are given instantly. It is good practice to determine exactly what is essential and therefore needs to be immediately accessible. Any tools or equipment that are used infrequently can go into more permanent storage or – blasphemous words – be disposed of.

A workstation is useful for containing the build and preventing it from spreading to unwanted areas. This workstation was built for me by my father when I was a child, and still sees significant use today.

ESSENTIAL SUMMARY

- A workstation contains a project and makes it easier to organise, clean and move the project to other locations.
- Storage bins and organisers are an efficient way of ensuring that small bits and pieces do not get lost.
- There are many qualities to look for in a toolbox – consider them all before purchase.
- No matter what you do, a toolbox will always be filled...

Health and Safety Gear

Health and safety gear can seem excessive and unnecessary, and, in a moment of frustration or urgency, is easy to overlook. A 'better safe than sorry' approach, however, will mean a few seconds putting on a pair of safety glasses could avert a trip to the hospital.

Safety Glasses

Safety glasses protect the eyes from all forms of projectile. Glasses should be used in any situation where material is propelled into the air, which could include using a saw, working with material from below a surface or sanding. It is always important to think not only about the immediate hazards but also the long-term effects. Take sanding, for example: constantly getting sawdust or grit in the eyes will not benefit your health long term.

Masks

A mask is essential when working with spray paints, airbrushing or any other form of aerosol. While it may be tempting to go for the face masks with the elastic band that often come in a cheaper multi-pack, it is much better to acquire a quality respirator. These come with changeable filters, meaning the mask itself does not need replacement unless it becomes damaged. Certain filters can only be used for a specific purpose, so check on this on the product description.

A selection of essential health and safety equipment. When in doubt, put it on – there is no sense in taking unnecessary risks.

Scalpel Blade Disposal

It is good practice to have some form of container in which to dispose of old scalpel blades. You can buy scalpel blade removers, some with containers attached. If this is not feasible, simply get a glass jar and cover the open top with some heavy-duty tape with a slit cut in the middle.

ESSENTIAL SUMMARY

- It is always better to be safe than sorry.
- Use safety glasses whenever working with sharp objects, including any materials that could shatter and cause injury.
- A respirator should be used when working with aerosol paints.
- Take the time to dispose of old blades properly – failing to do this can cause injury to others.

Materials

The following list of materials is far from exhaustive, but those mentioned have been selected for their relative ease of use and accessibility. Most can be found at local hobby shops, art stores or popular online sites, and any technical equipment that may be required beyond the basic toolset is fairly inexpensive.

An assortment of common scratch-building materials. These are often integrated into kit-bashing builds to add extra detail – often where repeated shapes and forms are needed.

Wood

Wood is an organic, porous material. It is used in a variety of situations, from structural frames and baseboards to miniature props and furniture. The form wood comes in depends upon the application. Sheet material can be found ranging from small lengths of 30cm (12in) up to 8 × 4ft (2.4 × 1.2m) flats (sheets) and above. Edging, strips and trim can be obtained in profiles that vary in much the same way.

There are two main types of wood: hardwood and softwood. The general rule is exactly what it says on the tin; hardwood is denser and typically harder than softwood. However, there are exceptions. The most notable of these is balsa, which, despite being technically a hardwood, is amazingly soft and one of the most popular woods for model making. It is lightweight, cheap and easy to work with.

There are many different species of wood ('species' denoting it comes from living trees), all with their individual qualities. Common examples include oak, walnut and obeche. Then there is a selection of man-made woods, which have noticeably different qualities from their natural counterparts. One of the most common is MDF, which, with its smooth surface and high density, is superb as a construction material. An eco-friendlier variant of this is Wheatboard, or Ecoboard.

Working with wood typically involves equipment and adhesives that will very quickly become familiar, including scalpels and saws. The density of wood will often dictate which is to be used, which will in turn also influence the use of materials such as specific grades of sandpaper. When working with thin strips of wood and cutting at an angle, a mitre block is advisable. As wood is a porous material, it tends to soak up adhesive, meaning that thicker consistencies work better. Wood glue is the go-to, being a thicker PVA in most cases. Superglue should be avoided as it will rarely form a strong bond and will ruin any stains or wood dye finishes on the surface.

There are several key tips to working efficiently with wood. Firstly, care should be taken to keep the surface clean. An awareness of which direction the grain is running (the stripes you see in the surface) is crucial when cutting, as going against the grain is much more difficult than going with the grain. Wood is prone to snapping, so a supporting structure may be required in some cases. Arguably, the most important thing to be aware of is storage. Wood warps, meaning it bends and twists, which can in many cases prove difficult or impossible to rectify. This occurs when the moisture content changes, so it is essential to store wood in a clean, dry environment.

A cigarette lighter case made using styrene. Thin moulded strips of styrene, though expensive, make detailing much quicker.

Styrene

Styrene, also known as Plasticard and high-impact polystyrene, is a plastic. It can be used in wargaming, architectural modelling and vacuum forming (where it is heated and pressed over an object to form a replica). There are typically two main forms: sheets and pre-formed strips. Styrene can be found in varying sheet sizes and thicknesses, commonly ranging from 0.5mm to 2mm (0.02–0.08in). Pre-formed strips often come in rectangular lengths of 30cm to a metre (12–40in), though other shapes include I-beams, T-beams, rods, quarters, half-rounds and more.

Styrene varies little in terms of substance. It can be found in a range of colours, most frequently black and white. The surface is typically smooth, although various moulded textures can be obtained in sheet form, most commonly brickwork and cladding. These are moulded to scale, which should be noted prior to purchase.

The primary tools for working with styrene are scalpels, steel rulers and a cutting mat. Saws should be avoided, as it is easy to crack the styrene surface and doing so will often chew up the blade. Styrene can be easily sanded, though it is best to do this by hand – using a sanding machine will generate heat, which could cause the plastic to deform. A safety ruler is advisable, as the smooth surface of the styrene means that, should the knife jump at any point, there is little friction to stop it travelling far.

Styrene can be glued using a range of adhesives. Styrene-to-styrene bonding is best achieved using plastic welding glue. This has a water-like consistency and will neatly weld the two pieces together; so neatly, in fact, that any marks are rarely noticeable after painting. This will be explained in more detail in Chapter 2.

The biggest tip to be aware of with styrene is that it should not be cut. Regardless of the thickness, styrene can be scored lightly with a blade and then, with a small amount of pressure, be bent and snapped. This results in a nice clean edge. Cutting through thicker sheets will leave a burr (raised edge), which is often unsightly and becomes particularly noticeable after the application of a wash (*see* Chapter 2). This can be removed, however, through the use of a scribing tool. Sanding should be avoided in this scenario to ensure that the smooth surface of the styrene is unblemished.

Foamboard

Foamboard is a lightweight sheet material. It consists of three layers: a layer of what is essentially styrofoam sandwiched between two layers of thick paper. It is frequently used in display mounting and architectural modelling, though its application is diverse, including sculpting and shaping underlying structures for terrain. Sheets of foamboard tend to be quite large, around A2 to A1 sizes, and is typically 2–10mm (0.08–0.4in) thick.

KAPA is a specific type of foamboard with a much denser core, typically cream in colour. With standard foamboard, the paper layers cannot be peeled away neatly and without damaging the underlying foam. With KAPA, the paper can be removed in one neat piece to expose the centre layer. The denser foam can be sculpted into, retaining any impressions that are made, meaning its application is more diverse.

Foamboard is most often cut with a scalpel to avoid damaging the centre layer of foam. Cutting foamboard is one of the best ways to expose a blunt blade, as the foam will be torn off in small chunks instead of retaining a crisp, neat edge. White or black foamboard should not be sanded, as this tends to destroy the surface; however, sanding is perfectly fine with KAPA and is often an ideal way to shape it. To join foamboard, it's best to use water-based adhesive, as solvent-based products will dissolve the foam and create a cavity, leaving little to no bond.

Working with foamboard effectively is essentially a list of what to avoid as opposed to what to do. Do not store other things on top of or around it, as the edges and corners are prone to damage, and once the layers of paper are creased or dented, that's it! Do not start cutting with a blade that has been used substantially. In fact, best practice is to use a fresh blade when working with foamboard. One of the most common issues is cutting through to the last layer of paper and then giving in to the temptation to bend and tear it. This is incredibly wasteful and almost always fails as the paper will tear further across the surface of the board. Take the time to cut through it completely and perfectly.

Cardboard

This is one of the most common materials encountered in daily life and, as such, varies immensely in terms of texture and composition. Cardboard can range from thin coloured card typically used in packaging or for crafting to the brown corrugated cardboard used for packaging. Mountboard is another popular variant, used often in picture framing, although grey mountboard is a fairly common variant used in concept modelling.

Cardboard is lightweight, flexible and, when arranged into a structure, can become incredibly strong. Often dismissed as an 'unprofessional' material, when used properly, cardboard can satisfy many criteria. Combined with its ease of acquisition, which is often free, and its position as one of the most eco-friendly materials available, its versatility is the reason particular consideration should be given to cardboard and is why it frequently appears in this book.

Working with card is often more complex than first imagined. Thin card, such as is used to make cereal boxes, can be easily cut with a pair of scissors, although a scalpel blade is always recommended. Brown corrugated card is much stronger and better suited to construction. Both types are relatively flexible and can be used to create curved forms, but corrugated card will only flex one way and can crease more easily. Another disadvantage to using corrugated card is revealed when it comes to gluing. The holes along the edge allow glue to push up into the material when it is pressed against another surface. This leaves only a small surface area to adhere to, which is why a hot glue gun is advisable. When using thinner card, a wood glue or PVA will suffice.

Cleaning: the number one tip for working with card. Keeping the surface smooth as well as neatening any joining areas is a priority. When two pieces of card are joined together with PVA, the glue will be squeezed out and start to drip. Having a damp cloth or cotton bud to hand will mean these overspills can be quickly cleaned and a neat, professional finish achieved.

Another important element to prepare for is painting. Painted cardboard will warp, and preparation for this begins during construction. Supporting beams across the reverse surface (whichever side is not being seen) will help to prevent this issue, as will using adhesives such as hot glue or double-sided tape – watery PVA can be just as bad as paint. As with foamboard, card should be protected as much as possible, as the edges and corners can be damaged very easily. Planning should also go into determining how much cardboard is going to be used, as the thicker variants can become much heavier than previously thought when layered together.

PVC Foam

PVC (polyvinyl chloride) foam is actually more akin to a plastic. It is generally used for signage and display boards due to its light weight and durability. Sheets of PVC foam can be found in all colours and sizes. The surface is often slightly textured and the edges can feel quite rough, but its effectiveness as a construction material has led to it becoming extremely popular.

PVC foam is strangely satisfying to cut as it feels quite spongey when using a scalpel – a lot less effort is required than you may think at first. PVC foam can be glued using a number of products. Superglue is particularly effective, although wood glue can also work well. The solid edge means that very little adhesive will be absorbed or wasted – and therefore very little is required in the first place.

There are few specific tips and techniques for working with PVC foam as it is such a simple material to use. There is no central layer to damage, the corners and edges are more resilient to wear than on other materials, and its flexible and durable surface cannot be creased. The main point to be aware of is that, although PVC foam is light relative to its strength, any substantial structures built with this material can become surprisingly heavy.

Due to the chemicals used in the production of PVC foam, it is arguably not the most eco-friendly of materials, however. Using offcuts or salvaged pieces saved from landfill is to be encouraged, but when looking to buy new material, other options should be considered as well.

Styrofoam

Styrofoam is a light blue foam. It typically comes in large, thick sheets or blocks, although thinner material, with a depth of just a few millimetres, is available as well. It is not to be mistaken for polystyrene foam, which is the white packaging material that joyously showers the room in tiny white pellets on Christmas Day. Styrofoam is commonly used for insulation in construction, although it has also found popularity in the wargaming community as a useful material for making terrain.

Depending on its thickness, styrofoam may require more technical equipment than is typically found in the standard toolbox. Thin sheets can be easily cut with a scalpel, although a longer blade and handle may improve control. Substantially thicker sheets or blocks will require the use of a hot wire cutter that glides through the foam and enables the user to sculpt the surface. The choice of adhesive follows similar guidelines as for foamboard. Any solvent-based product will likely destroy

the surface of the styrofoam, though the effect is typically less severe than that on regular foamboard. Epoxy resin is an effective choice, though more preparation is required beforehand.

Styrofoam often requires substantial investment. It is at the more expensive end of the scale in terms of pure cost of materials, and, depending on the dimensions, may also require investment in equipment such as a hot wire cutter. Epoxy resin can be tricky to work with, especially for a beginner model maker, so thorough research and experimentation is advised before working on the final model. To avoid waste, it is best when sculpting to mark out the desired shape using a permanent marker and then to choose a piece of material as close to those dimensions as possible.

This bench build uses a combination of scratch-building and kit-bashing processes. The main bench structure is scratch built from obeche wood, whilst the cushions are made from sponge cloth and kitchen roll (a technique covered in Chapter 7).

ESSENTIAL SUMMARY

- An understanding of material will improve your understanding of adhesives, paints and more.
- Cost should only factor into a decision if a material is unaffordable. Never choose a material based on the theory that 'more expensive is better'.
- Most materials can be made to imitate others with the correct techniques, so choose a material based upon qualities other than just aesthetics.
- It is always a good idea to source a little sample of each material and experiment with constructing some basic forms with it. Learn through practice as well as planning.

Paints and Finishes

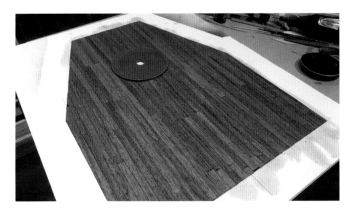

A wooden floor made during my final year at university. The natural finish to the flooring was achieved by staining the floorboards and then jumbling them up before adhering to the baseboard. This creates a more realistic colour variation in the wood.

The deck of a Tamiya *Hornet* has been masked to create a clean edge. Although masking is time consuming, it is worth every second spent for the final crisp line it achieves. An airbrush is recommended.

Preparation

A successful finish to a build depends as much upon the preparation of the model as it does technical skill. Keeping a model clean, protective materials close by, and simply being aware of the surface the model is resting on can avoid significant issues when it comes to painting.

Keeping the Model Clean

All sorts of materials get deposited on the surface of a model as it is constructed. Oil and grease from our hands is an immediate issue, though this can be easily prevented by putting on a pair of gloves (check the material if you suffer from sensitive skin or allergies, or if you are using solvent-based products).

Filling and Sanding

Any gaps, scratches or uneven areas should be treated with some filler or putty. Putty tends to shrink after application, but filler usually requires more sanding, so bear this in mind before application.

In contrast, a very smooth surface means certain paints will not adhere well, which often manifests over a significant period through chipping or peeling. It is therefore important to sand the surface of the model, using either sandpaper sheets or sanding blocks, to give the paint something to 'grip' onto.

When choosing sandpaper, pay attention to the grade – how rough the sandpaper is. The lower the number, the rougher the sandpaper; at the other end of the scale, this number can go up into the thousands, where the sandpaper actually polishes the surface. Start with a lower grade and work up until the desired surface texture is achieved. For most jobs, a good rule of thumb is to work up to whichever grade removes any visible scratches from the model.

Work Surface

Ideally, one should paint a model on a turntable, so the maker can sit in one position and rotate the turntable to paint the model from all sides. Ensure the work surface is covered in a protective material – any spillages will be much easier to clean.

Paints

Acrylic

Acrylics come in a huge range of colours and are one of the most common types of paint. They are water-based, meaning they can be thinned and cleaned with water, and quick-drying, which can work both for and against the user; acrylic mediums can alter this.

Acrylic paint adheres best to smooth surfaces, but do not paint over the top of oil paint, as it will flake off. Bear in mind also that the finish is not waterproof.

Oil

Oil paints can be thinned and washed with a variety of solvent-based solutions – most commonly thinners and mineral spirits. Do not clean oil paints in water. Solvents release harmful vapours, so wear a mask.

When a tube of oil paint is opened, typically there is a small amount of oil pooled at the top. A useful tip is to squeeze the paint onto a piece of kitchen roll instead of a palette, as the kitchen roll will absorb the oil, ensuring that it is not transferred onto the model.

Enamels

Enamel paints are generally oil-based so require solvents to thin and clean.

They need to be mixed prior to use, but enamel paint is hard-wearing and forms a waterproof layer, meaning it is very popular with model boat enthusiasts.

Powders

Model-making powders often come in small jars or in the form of weathering palettes. They can be mixed and cleaned using water to create various streaking and weathering effects.

Powders need to be sealed under a thin layer of varnish, however, otherwise they will smudge and fade when handled.

Paint for Airbrushing

Only water-based paints should be used with an airbrush. While it is possible to use oil paints, not only will they require extra cleaning but more harmful vapours will be released into the air. There is a large range of ready mixed paint optimised for airbrushing available on the market. These come in very small bottles, which can dissuade newcomers to airbrushing, as they seem expensive for their size. However, a little goes a long way, so a small bottle will cover a relatively large area.

If you do not intend to use ready-mixed paint, ensure the solution is of the consistency of ink. Too thick and the paint will clog up the airbrush; too thin and it will run. Keep an eye on the solution while painting, as there is the possibility, depending on what has been used, that the mixture could separate.

> **ESSENTIAL SUMMARY**
>
> - Water-based paints can be thinned and cleaned with water. Oil-based paints require washing with mineral spirits or equivalent solvents.
> - Oil paint can be painted on top of acrylic, but acrylic should not be painted on top of oil as it will flake off.
> - Enamels require mixing before use.
> - Apply powders in small amounts and be wary of any debris falling onto unwanted areas of the model.

There are so many different types of paint out there that this is only a small selection of what is available.

Airbrushing

Airbrushing is a spray-paint technique that has become immensely popular due to the airbrush's ability to create clean, even layers of paint and superior blending compared to a traditional paintbrush.

In order to start airbrushing, several items are needed other than the airbrush itself, and it is important to invest in these items all at once if this is an appealing prospect. Many of the issues encountered with airbrushing can be resolved simply by having the appropriate materials immediately to hand.

There are two main criteria to first be aware of when looking for an airbrush to purchase:

- Is it single or dual action?
- Is it siphon or gravity feed?

Single or Double?

When the trigger is pressed on a single-action airbrush, air and paint are released simultaneously (just like with a spray can). 'Double action' means that the trigger separates these functions: just pressing down only releases air, and the paint is then released by pulling the trigger. The further the trigger is pulled back, the more paint is released. This may seem more complicated, but with some practice leads to a more efficient workflow.

Siphon or Gravity?

Siphon and gravity feed refer to where the paint is drawn from. Siphon feed means that paint is first mixed in a small jar, which is then attached below the airbrush nozzle. The paint is then siphoned (drawn up) through the airbrush.

Gravity feed means that paint is poured into a cap that sits on top of the airbrush, and it is simply pulled down through the airbrush by gravity.

There are pros and cons to both methods. With siphon feed, paint pots can be prepared easily in advance and stored after use, but these airbrushes can be trickier to clean. Gravity feed is a much simpler method, but for every colour change the cap has to be emptied and cleaned thoroughly, which can be time-consuming and waste paint.

The Needle

The needle is the backbone of the airbrush and controls how much air and paint is released. It does this by first blocking the airbrush nozzle (if you look closely, you will see a tiny sharp point sticking out). This is why the nozzle is so important – not only does it help to direct the paint, but it prevents injury.

Needles have to be removed from the airbrush for a change-over or for cleaning. It is of vital importance that the tip of the needle does not touch anything when removed, as it is extremely fragile. Make sure that a clean and even surface is prepared on which to place the needle, and that the needle cannot roll off it.

Cleaning

The most important rule with using an airbrush is to keep it clean. Almost every problem a user will encounter with it will arise from poor maintenance. It is essential to ensure that after every use the airbrush is cleaned thoroughly and kept as close to mint condition as possible.

Such is the importance of this, here is a quick guide on cleaning a gravity-fed airbrush at the end of the day. For a simple colour change mid-use, only steps one to three are really necessary.

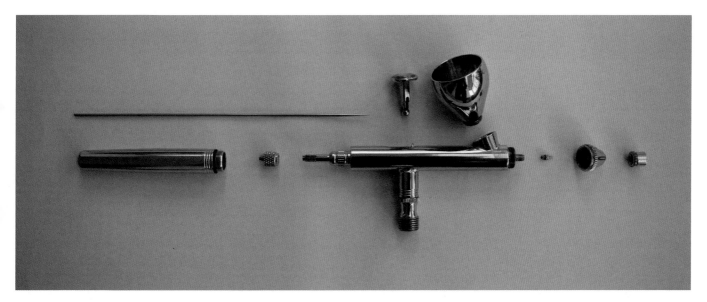

Airbrushes are made up of various components and often require disassembly. Familiarising yourself with these components will make the process less daunting and ensure that they are properly maintained.

1. Deal with leftover paint. If a significant amount of paint is remaining, pour it out into a container. Otherwise, start by using a paper towel to wipe out as much paint from the cap as possible.

Cleaning an airbrush: step 1.

2. Pour a small amount of airbrush-cleaning solution into the cap. Use a paintbrush to mix any stubborn paint into the solution but do not press too firmly to avoid damaging the needle. Tip the solution out onto some paper towel. Do not use water to clean an airbrush, as it will cause spluttering and will not remove as much paint as airbrush-cleaning solution.

Cleaning an airbrush: Step 2.

3. Add another small amount of cleaning solution to the cap, but this time spray the solution out into a cleaning pot. Airbrush cleaning pots are an essential tool for airbrushing as they contain both a stand and a filter, which means less spillage and fewer harmful vapours being released into the air.

Cleaning an airbrush: Step 3.

4. Separate the needle and nozzle. This requires a small amount of disassembly. Unscrew the airbrush casing to reveal the needle. Next, unscrew the knob that clamps the trigger mechanism to the needle. Slowly and carefully, draw the needle out. Keep the needle in your hand at all times to avoid any damage.

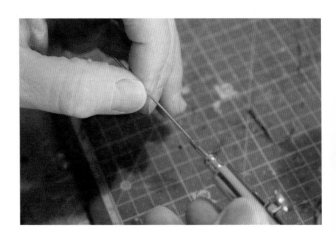

Cleaning an airbrush: Step 4.

5. Take a cotton bud and soak the end in cleaning solution. Ever so gently, drag it along the needle in one direction only – towards the tip. Dragging it the other way would risk damaging the tip. Repeat until clean.

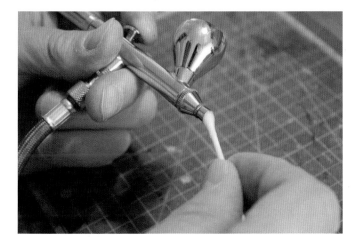

Cleaning an airbrush: Step 6.

6. For the nozzle, again take a cotton bud soaked in solution. Clean the outer side of the cap, which will have a small build-up of paint. Use a small paintbrush soaked in solution to clean the inside. Reassemble and, for good measure, add a tiny amount of cleaning solution to the cap and spray through a final time.

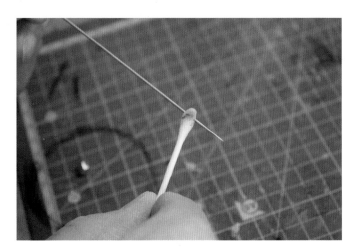

Cleaning an airbrush: Step 5.

The Compressor

The compressor generates the air needed for the airbrush to function. Compressors come in all shapes and sizes, but the most important information to look for is the psi – pounds per square inch – which refers to pressure. The higher the pressure, the more forcefully the paint will come out of the airbrush. Around 20psi is good for airbrushing, but there is no fixed value – the ideal pressure depends upon several factors, including the mixture of the paint. Most compressors will come with a pressure gauge so it is not a guessing game.

An alternative to using a compressor is to purchase airbrush propellant canisters, which look similar to cans of spray paint. The airbrush is connected to the canister in the same way as a compressor, but there is no need for electricity. While this allows for more flexibility, propellant canisters are not cost-effective in the long run.

Preventing Splutter

Spluttering occurs when paint accumulates on the end of the airbrush needle or nozzle, when dry paint starts clogging the mechanism, or when the air pressure is too low. The result is splatters of paint on the model's surface that can ruin the final paint finish.

Reducing the risk of paint drying and clogging the nozzle is therefore a priority, and the best way to do this is through the mixing ratio of the paint. A good mix, based on experience is given below:

- 10 drops of paint, ideally ready-mixed airbrush paint such as Vallejo Model Air
- 4 drops of thinner, again ideally optimised for airbrushing
- 2 drops of flow improver

List of Materials

A number of products will make using an airbrush much easier and far more pleasant:

Compressor – Keep in mind power – the more power, the more noise!
Cleaning pot – Comes with a stand and filtered compartment, making it especially useful for cleaning
Paints – Ideally go for ready-mixed paints to save time. Do not be dissuaded by the seemingly expensive miniature bottles – a little goes a long way with airbrushing

Airbrush cleaner – Essential for cleaning
Airbrush thinner – To help the paint flow through the airbrush
Airbrush flow improver – To help prevent paint drying on the needle and to assist the flow of paint through the airbrush.

ESSENTIAL SUMMARY

- Keeping the airbrush clean is the number one priority.
- Hold the airbrush like a pen, with the index finger on the trigger and the thumb and middle fingers gripping below.
- Always have a cleaning pot or stand ready, even if its homemade, to ensure that when the airbrush is set down, any remaining paint does not spill.
- Practice makes perfect – airbrushing is not instant but it is quick to learn.

Gluing

Preparation

The correct choice of adhesive can make or break a model. It can either form a solid bond for years on end or it can fail to bond at all, even going so far as to actively ruin the materials being used. But the correct adhesive must be accompanied with correct practice.

Cleaning

Work spaces must be clean for all parts of a project; a messy work space will present two issues.

The first is that clutter will make it difficult to apply adhesive with any real finesse and, should there be any spillages, tools and equipment can quickly be ruined. The second is that untidy workstations usually mean dust and debris. Dusty surfaces can prevent the adhesive from forming a strong bond and debris can stop two pieces joining correctly.

Zones

It is good practice to divide the work area into zones so that an efficient production line can be formed. These zones can include:

- A glue-preparation area, where certain adhesives can be dispensed into containers for ease of application
- An area for dirty tools, such as those that will make contact with the adhesive. These should be isolated to ensure that the glue is not transferred onto unwanted objects, even if this means just folding up some newspaper on which to rest equipment
- Cleaning materials – water, sprays, sponges, cloths, gloves and so on

Heat

Adhesives prefer warmer environments to facilitate the drying process. Cold rooms result in glue taking a long time to dry, which increases the risk of unwanted movement. This does not necessarily mean turning a heater onto full – room temperature is more than satisfactory.

Common Sense

Common sense goes a long way when working with adhesives. Ensure the room is well-ventilated before using hazardous substances, ensure that the floor is clear should a mad dash for cleaning materials prove essential (we have all been there) and last, but certainly not least – roll your sleeves up and tie your hair back!

Application

Only add the amount of adhesive that is required: too little, and the materials simply will not stick; too much, and the glue will take a long time to dry. If the materials do not bond initially, refrain from applying even more adhesive, which just results in a sludgy mess. Remove the initial layer of adhesive as much as possible before applying a second.

Nozzles

Nozzles result in more controlled application, but are prone to blocking. Ensure that the nozzle is thoroughly cleaned after every application.

Drying

Avoid touching a model as much as possible while the adhesive is drying. Tools such as engineer's squares and clamps are vital for holding components of a model together as they bond. Elastic bands can be used in some situations, but they are unreliable and can just as easily damage a model.

Dust and debris can affect a model in many ways. An additional precaution to take when the model is drying is to cover it with some newspaper, tin foil or fabric.

Packing up

Once the bond has cured (reached its maximum strength), clean up all tools and equipment immediately. Depending on how long they have been left in the first place and the type of adhesive that has been used, this may require more substantial care, such as soaking in warm, soapy water. The glue itself should be stored away from harsh sunlight and areas of notable heat – some glues, such as superglue, prefer to be kept in the fridge.

ESSENTIAL SUMMARY

- Prepare well in advance to avoid costly accidents.
- Ensure the space is reasonably warm to facilitate the drying process.
- Avoid applying glue directly from a bottle.
- Do not disturb the model as it dries – resist the urge to meddle!

Adhesives

In the world of model making, there are just as many adhesives as there are materials, and seeing all of the different types can be a little overwhelming. For the texture samples in Part II,

almost every example uses PVA glue as it is a common adhesive that most people are aware of and is easily accessible. However, PVA will not suit every scenario. It is vital, before starting any project, to have a firm understanding of the following:

- What materials will be used
- Which adhesives bond the chosen materials
- Which adhesives will bond opposing materials
- Setting and curing times
- Safety precautions

Drying and Curing Times

This often catches people off-guard in that there is a distinct difference between a glue that is dry and a glue that is cured.

'Drying time' refers to how long it takes until the adhesive is no longer a liquid and can be touched – commonly known as 'touch dry'. Once an adhesive has dried, work can usually resume on a model as long as it is not too delicate. This is because it may not have cured yet.

'Curing time' is how long it takes for the adhesive to reach its strongest state, and is considerably longer than the drying time. Even after an adhesive is dry enough to work with, a reaction is still taking place. For example, hot glue from a glue gun will become touch dry rather quickly but still remain quite weak for a time; weak enough for the adhered materials to come apart if placed under strain. A little more time is needed for the adhesive to harden fully and reach its full strength.

These times vary across each and every product, and they are significantly affected by the conditions they are placed in. The colder a room is, for example, the longer it usually takes for an adhesive to dry and cure. Therefore there is no mention of timings in the following descriptions – instead, read the label and factor in the conditions in which the adhesive will be used.

PVA

PVA (polyvinyl acetate) bonds porous surfaces, including paper, card, cardboard and certain fabrics. It will rarely bond any plastic or metal materials.

PVA glue can be cleaned off with warm water.

Pros Very safe, easy to use, readily available, dries clear, cheap
Cons Not the strongest bond and will only adhere porous materials

Glue Stick

Glue sticks are more sustainable as they can be water-based and made almost entirely from natural ingredients, such as potato starch. They will bond porous materials together, but typically limited to just card and paper.

As the glue is already in a partially solid state, it tends to be difficult to clean off and can leave persistent marks on any surface.

Pros Accessible, cheap and easy to use
Cons One of the most limited and weakest adhesives

UHU

This all-purpose adhesive will bond many different types of materials. It is best suited to bonding porous surfaces, but will also tackle some plastics and metals.

UHU should be treated as a contact adhesive, in that both faces should be covered in a layer of glue, left to go tacky, and then pressed together.

One of the main things to avoid with UHU is squeezing the tube. Many a student has done this only to find nothing coming out, and so squeezed a little more only to recoil in horror as the entire contents empty out onto the model. Hold the tube straight up and let gravity do the work.

Pros Will bond a wide range of materials and is relatively cheap compared to buying specific individual adhesives
Cons Difficult to control and can create a mess.

Superglue

Superglue is simply the household name for cyanoacrylate. This is an effective adhesive for bonding surfaces such as styrene, foamed PVC and household plastics, but avoid using it on fabrics, polystyrene and foamboard, as it could physically damage them.

Pros Very strong, can bond many materials and is quick acting
Cons Relatively expensive, potentially harmful and leaves little room for error

Plastic Weld

Plastic weld is ideally suited to bonding styrene. Instead of forming a solid adhesive layer, the glue will flow between the two materials and soften the surface areas in contact with one another – thus welding them together.

Plastic weld can release quite noxious fumes, however, so requires the use of a respirator.

Pros Ultra quick-drying, very easy to apply and forms the neatest adhesive bond from this selection
Cons Perhaps too quick-drying for those not familiar with this application method

Hot Glue

Hot glue will bond most materials, both porous and non-porous. It is applied with a glue gun, and should not be applied in thin layers, as it will simply dry too quickly.

Pros Quick-drying, cheap, and can be used in moulding and casting
Cons Very weak, can be too quick-drying and carries an increased risk of burns

Epoxy

Using epoxy requires mixing two components before use: the resin – the bulk of the adhesive – and a hardener. When the hardener is added to the resin, it will start an exothermic reaction (one that releases heat).

Epoxy forms an extremely strong bond and is best used for adhering materials that most other glues struggle with, for example metals, ceramic and rubber.

Pros Very strong bond, adheres most materials other glues struggle with
Cons Many health and safety risks and often messy

A collection of adhesives. As with paint, there is a huge range available on the market, with even the same types having their own individual characteristics between manufacturers.

CHAPTER 3

PROFESSIONAL PRACTICE

This section covers several key elements of the model-making process that will contribute greatly to the professional execution of a project.

Professional practice is what separates a beginner from an expert. In the case of model making, it is being aware of the process as opposed to the object. Anyone can learn the differences between materials, or how a certain piece of equipment should be used, but only the most invested will dedicate the time needed to refine their craft.

In many instances, what makes a professional is often assumed and goes without saying, lying either firmly in the realm of common sense or knowledge that has been passed between generations through pure observation (for example, accounting for the width of the pencil lead when marking along a ruler). This can be frustrating, as those who are new to the craft must take the time to discover these things – which greatly streamline workflow and improves quality – for themselves.

Self-discovery is crucial to ensure that ever-rewarding satisfaction that fuels our love of model making. However, assumptions in knowledge create gaps, and as teachers (which all model makers are, whether they know it or not), it should be our responsibility to fill these gaps.

Changing a Scalpel Blade

Starting with one of the basics, changing a scalpel blade safely and efficiently saves both time and injury. While there are many devices that will assist in the removing of scalpel blades, these require additional investment. The method described below applies to virtually any hobby knife and utilises tools that should already be in a standard toolkit.

1. Holding the scalpel away from the body, take a pair of pliers and grab the base of the blade. Do not grab the blade's point as there is a risk of the end snapping.
2. Push the blade off the handle and dispose of it safely.
3. Take the new blade, again holding the base with the pliers.
4. Push the new blade onto the handle, still keeping it pointing away from the body. In the case of a Swann-Morton, there should be a satisfying click.

Changing a scalpel blade: step 1.

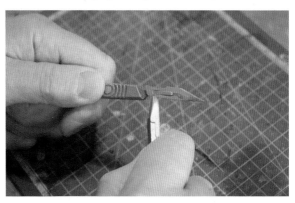

Changing a scalpel blade: step 2.

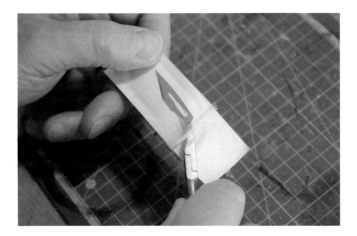

Changing a scalpel blade: step 3.

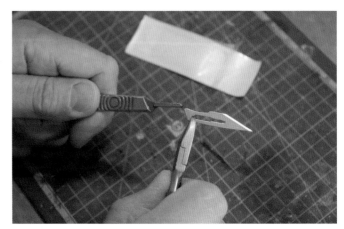

Changing a scalpel blade: step 4.

This may sound like basic common sense, but it is not at all unusual to see people attempting to remove blades with their fingers or adopting equally unsafe practices. As dangerous as this can be when removing a scalpel blade, placing one back on unsafely can be even more so. In fact, failing to install a blade correctly often leads to it being unstable, thus increasing the risk of the blade snapping.

There are many different blade types for the Swann-Morton, each with its specific purpose. The 10A is the blade with which most will already be familiar, but practice with several to get a feel for which blades are appropriate for the task at hand.

Optimising your Time

For many, model making is a hobby, meaning deadlines are rarely of much concern. However, many a model has fallen victim to the 'I will build it one day' pile. Simple time-optimisation techniques can assist in combatting this problem. For professionals, of course, managing time effectively is essential.

Production Line

Setting up a production line can greatly speed up the process of completing one major project or several projects all at once. The best approach for this is to separate the build into three defined stages:

Stage 1 – Construction Working on multiple projects at the same time can take a little of the fun out of it, but it massively saves time packing everything away and then unpacking once more. If several projects have been started, have a defined area for them or, better yet, a container that can be worked out of. A tray is ideal for this, as it creates a separate area, it confines all of one model to that area naturally and can be easily moved if more space is needed at any time.

Stage 2 – Painting This is where most time can be saved in practice. Especially if paints are being mixed, setting up a production line for this stage is nigh on essential. Even for one project, priming, airbrushing and weathering components all at the same time saves on wastage and cleaning. It also has the added bonus of ensuring that a level of consistency is maintained. It is incredibly frustrating to be satisfied with a certain technique or finish only to then be unable to recall how that finish was achieved for the next component.

Stage 3 – Finishing Whether this is weathering, creating a base or adding scenic elements, finishing often involves a lot of materials, and packing and unpacking everything that is required can be very time-consuming. Try to save builds for this stage so that they can be tackled en masse. This will also allow you to tackle material usage more efficiently. You don't want to use all the best bits on one model and be left with just scraps for the next.

The benefits to this approach are numerous:

- All the necessary tools are out at the same time.
- No unnecessary tools clutter the workspace.
- The same effect or finish can be easily applied to numerous areas at once.

- The modeller can make the most of good conditions, for example hot weather.
- Fewer clothes will be ruined...

What to do When Pieces are Drying

The usual answer to this would be to have a cup of tea. However, there should always be tasks left for when parts of a build require drying time. These include:

Tidying and cleaning – Keeping on top of the workstation can save time and prevent an even bigger end-of-project clean-up. Most studios have a big tidy at the end of every single day.

Preparing for the next stage – Swap out tools and equipment, gathering materials and figuring out the next stage.

Working on another project – A production line does not necessarily mean working on each project at the same time at the same stage. Another option is to get to the painting stage on the first, then to move onto the construction stage of the second as the paint dries. This is more of a domino approach.

Samples – If a particularly satisfactory finish or effect has been achieved, use the time while it is drying to make a small sample of this for the record, or write down the process. This saves the frustration of forgetting for future projects.

Measuring

Measure twice, cut once: this may be an age-old saying but it is just as relevant today, and it is amazing how many fall victim to the consequences of hasty measurements. This does not mean draw a line with a ruler and then stare at the measurement for an extra ten seconds just to take it in – it means literally measure twice. Draw the line, then take the ruler away completely. Realign everything and record the measurement once more. This is the effective way of identifying errors.

Mistakes can be further reduced by creating a cutting list beforehand. This is a physical list of all the components that are required for a build, including measurements and what material they will use. This helps to clarify measurements in

moments of confusion and reduce waste, as all of the components can be measured onto one sheet of material at once.

Extra Length

Some rulers have a space from the end of the ruler to the zero where there are no units of measurement. Make sure to align the zero and not the end of the ruler itself otherwise the measurement will be inaccurate. Similarly, when using a tape measure, ensure that the hook (end) of the tape is secure. If it is loose, it will add extra length when pulled against a surface. Regardless of the equipment being used, ensure it is flat against the surface: even a paper crease can cause inaccuracy.

Scope for introducing error is not limited to the measuring device itself. The marking implement – pencil, pen or similar – can add unwanted gaps if the width of the tip is not accounted for. Do not align a ruler right on top of an edge or pre-made marks. Instead, leave a little gap so that it is the end of the pencil, not the edge of the ruler, that makes contact with the desired mark.

These may seem like tiny details, but even half a millimetre difference repeated several times over can lead to big offsets.

Scrap Material and Offcuts

A nice, big, clean piece of sheet material is always satisfying to use, but it can also be wasteful. It would be a shame, for example, to take a large piece of cardboard only to cut out a component the width of a finger. It is much more efficient to use any suitable scraps.

This can just as easily lead to other bad habits, such as hoarding, but it is important to maintain a collection of scrap material or offcuts for smaller jobs and to save larger sheet materials for bigger construction. This will ultimately save time – that would be spent breaking down the larger sheet into a workable section – and money, by making the most of materials already purchased.

When it comes to organisation, try to sort components by material and shape. Triangular shapes make great supports for walls or internal spaces, while curved pieces can be used to build up terrain. Anything with a straight edge should be kept for more visible, technical modelling. Whatever system you choose, ensure that pieces are divided up, purely to save time rummaging through one big pile.

Digital Models

Over the years, digital modelling has evolved exponentially and its benefit to physical modelling even more so. Preparing a digital model allows a model maker to effectively do a test run of the project, to double-check measurements and material quantities. It serves as an ideal reference point throughout construction as it offers a complete three-dimensional view. Custom plans can be derived from a digital model and can even be taken through to the 3D printing process.

Going through all of the available software and its potential applications would really require starting another book, but there are a few notable options worth mentioning:

SketchUp – A popular CAD program with a free online version (SketchUp Free) and a free desktop version (SketchUp Make 2017). Very easy for CAD beginners to learn

Blender – A free CAD program that offers additional animation and rendering capabilities for more advanced users

Fusion 360 – Ideal for engineering and product design

Recycling – Arguably the most accessible resource, household recycling yields a wealth of materials that are completely free. Remember that this extends beyond the personal household – recycling bins can be raided down the street on bin day so long as common courtesy is followed and the street remains tidy. It's always best to start with a friendly knock on the door…

Skips – I have worked with several colleagues who frequent skips regularly for materials. There are various health and safety implications with this and, if in doubt with regard to the general contents of the skip, avoid. However, if there are materials on the surface that have potential use, then just check with the owner or operator before removing. Again, simple common courtesy goes a long way and will often yield more results.

Contacting others – Broken electronics, old kits, general recycling – many forget to simply ask others for what they have available. What is junk to one person can be of great value to a model maker, and often helps out whoever is being asked by taking it off their hands. This can be extended to any local businesses going through a tech upgrade, for example.

Sourcing Materials

With regards to sourcing materials, professional practice is not about simply finding the best price, but making the most out of all available resources. Of course, some projects will simply require going to a shop or ordering large sheets of material online. Even in this instance, try to bulk buy to save on postage. Bulk buying also often reduces the chance of an individual purchase getting damaged, as bulk orders tend to be more substantially packaged. Ordering in bulk also helps to retain the same standard across all the purchased materials – buying sheets of wood in separate orders may result in slightly different shades, for example.

Whether or not the intention is to buy in bulk or in separate orders, it is important to make the most of all available resources, such as:

Online auctions – When kit bashing, old cameras, electronics and model kits are a great resource. Online auction sites, such as eBay, often sell job lots of these items and they are a great way of keeping costs down whilst acquiring a range of materials.

Angles

Do not assume that you can cut perfectly at a right angle or that purchased materials have been cut perfectly to size. There are many potential errors that can be made before any form of making has even begun, and identifying these can save confusion further down the line.

In making a cigarette lighter case prototype out of styrene, I found it essential to use a wooden template to align the pieces at the correct angles. A valuable lesson taught by my grandfather.

Sheet materials – These will come in predetermined sizes, but they are frequently a millimetre or so out. Also, edges may not meet perfectly at 90 degrees, so it is important to measure these prior to cutting. A simple check with an engineer's square will resolve this.

Strips – It is tempting to cut thin strips of material by eye, but this often leaves the end at an angle. Take the time to either measure both sides, no matter how far apart they are, to use an engineer's square or to use a mitre block. All three options will lead to a more accurate cut.

Edges – When using a scalpel to cut along the edge of a ruler, it is important to remember that the angle you hold the blade at will create a bevelled (angled) edge. For thin materials, such as paper or card, this rarely matters, but for foamboard this will make a huge difference. Keep the blade vertical and pressed against the edge of the ruler. It can be beneficial to stand up while doing this, as the arm can be straightened, giving more control.

Equipment Maintenance

Well-maintained equipment can last a lifetime. There will always be accidents or tactical trade-offs, but it is in the interest of model makers to maintain equipment to 'as new' standard wherever possible. Here are some simple measures everyone can take to greatly prolong a toolkit's lifespan:

Paintbrushes – Ruined paintbrushes are a common sight in any studio, but basic maintenance could have prevented this. Firstly, never leave a paintbrush tip down in water for prolonged periods, as this can deform the bristles. Secondly, ensure brushes are thoroughly cleaned after use. A quick swirl in water rarely does this – the exterior may look clean but the interior of the brush tip can still be clogged with paint. It is best to swirl first, wipe dry on a paper towel to open the bristles back up, then wash once more. Finally, store brushes away from dirt and dust. Popping them in a jar on the work surface is common but dust can quickly clog the bristles, which is subsequently transferred onto a model the next time those brushes are used. Storing your brushes in a wallet or a drawer is much better for them.

Equipment – IPA (isopropyl alcohol) is a great cleaning solution that will remove most substances from equipment. Test a small area first to ensure that no paint is lifted off or markings removed.

Cables – Good pieces of equipment can be ruined by broken or loose cables that are tripped over and send the equipment crashing to the floor. Maintenance in this regard is mostly preventative. Firstly, ensure that cables are kept well clear of any sharp objects or items that might otherwise damage them. Secondly, arrange cables through cable traps to keep them all neatly together and out of the way.

Spillages – Spilled superglue or other equally destructive substances can ruin a whole load of equipment in an instant. It follows that preventing spillages will help prolong the life of the majority of your toolkit. Ensure that lids are replaced and tightened. Place bottles in their own containers that will either prevent them from tipping over or constrain the spillage. Putting open bottles of superglue in an empty butter tub is one option. Additionally, place all of your tools onto a tray or removable surface so that, if spills do occur, they can all be moved out of the way in one quick movement.

Cloths – A simple damp cloth will go a long, long way in maintaining tools and equipment. Using a scalpel to cut through a component with glue on? Quickly wipe the blade on a damp cloth. Using an engineer's square to level up a painted surface that is still wet? Quickly wipe it with a damp cloth. Bit of dust on a sheet of styrene? You know the rest. Ensuring the cloth is damp will mean any residue or glue will not dry and leave streaks on surfaces.

ESSENTIAL SUMMARY

- As with many things, most professional practice is in the preparation.
- Work to maximise efficiency. Make the most of the time available.
- Maintenance is key to a smooth workflow.
- Use all available resources to gather supplies.

PART II: TECHNIQUES AND EFFECTS

CHAPTER 4

SCENERY

Scenery presents every model maker with an interesting challenge: to balance technical skill with natural credibility. We must ensure that we accurately replicate everything from a simple stone to an entire season while at the same time relinquishing enough control to make the scene appear natural; nothing can look forcibly placed.

Scenery concerns all of the natural elements of our project, from tiny lily pads on a village pond to mountainous ravines. We must research colour, season, geology, weather – in fact a lifetime can be spent amassing references without ever having enough.

This chapter looks at five techniques for creating common elements seen in all types of projects. The beauty is that these techniques can be used and adapted to create hundreds more, so the materials needed can be stretched an awfully long way. With landscaping such a significant part of their speciality, this will be of particular interest to railway modellers and wargamers.

Making Literacy

When planning scenic elements, we must think not only of individual textures but also how multiple textures interact with one another. Nature is formed through the collision of forces, leading to incredible variations. Points to consider include:

Shape – How has the landscape been formed? Has it been built up or destroyed over time? What force has done this? Has the weather changed your scenery and how will you represent this? How has it been affected by humans and animals?

Texture – There is no such thing as a 'grass texture'. Is it long or short? Straight or curved? Is it a grazing ground for animals – if so, is it badly damaged or nicely cultivated? How has the weather affected it? Do wild flowers grow among the blades?

Forces – What forces exert themselves in your scene? Running water? Rock falls? High winds? How are you going to portray this?

Your model – Scenery often forms many layers, which can add significant levels of weight to your scene. Will it be easy to move? Do you have a strong supporting structure? Scenery is easy to damage and very difficult to clean – how will you compensate for this?

GENERAL POINTS TO CONSIDER

- Think about the weather, which is often overlooked. An area prone to wet weather can benefit greatly from the addition of a gloss medium.
- If you are unhappy with the result of a certain technique, it is often difficult to remove, so ensure that you practise beforehand. Even so, to some degree the result will be out of your control.
- Never were photo references more applicable. Not only do we need visual references for each texture, but also for how it interacts with the surfaces around it.

When to Apply Scenic Elements

This can be a tough decision, as scenery often involves multiple stages of painting and adhesion. I would argue that the best time to apply scenery is once you have a sturdy, painted baseboard (always paint the base to ensure no bright colours shine through any gaps). Ensure that you have placed any key items in your scene before adding natural elements to properly base them. An old garden shed is often partially consumed by a hedge – hence the need to add the effect later. Some exceptions include characters. It is often best to add people to your scene while you are placing the scenery so they can make footprints, for example. Ultimately, this very much up comes down to individual judgment.

Water: Tissue Roll and PVA Glue

The tissue roll and PVA glue technique offers an incredibly realistic textured finish for little to no cost. When mixed with PVA glue, tissue forms into a paste-like substance that can be easily moulded and sculpted to your scene. Sheets can also be layered on top of a surface pre-coated in glue and subsequently stippled with a brush as an alternative way of texturing. With a substantial working time and solid finish (perfect for weathering), this technique gives you great flexibility.

> **MATERIALS AND EQUIPMENT**
>
> - Tissue roll
> - PVA glue
> - Paintbrush (this will likely become ruined, so use an old, stiff one)
> - Popsicle stick to mix the PVA and tissue roll into a paste
> - Container in which to mix the PVA and tissue roll
> - Tin foil (to put the tissue roll onto for better control before adding to your scene)
> - Water (to thin the glue slightly to create a more fluid medium if desired)

Pros

- Incredibly cheap technique; you will most likely have these materials to hand already
- Dries solid and, because of the addition of PVA, is very easy to paint over
- Additional materials can be easily added on top of the finished effect
- Long working time – no need to rush!

Cons

- You must be mindful of the material below warping if it's porous
- In colder weather, this process will take a long time to dry. Drying can be sped up with a hairdryer or heat gun

Tips and Tricks

- Gather together an assortment of tools and objects with which to add texture to the surface, as each will make their own distinctive marks.
- Tear the tissue roll into small pieces to help break it to down into a paste quicker.

Creating a water texture with tissue roll and PVA glue.

- If you do not like how the effect is looking, it can be scraped off the surface and reapplied.
- Start off with small amounts of glue – you can always add more as needed.

Step-by-Step Method

1. Start by cleaning the area where you want to apply the water texture. Ensure that the surface is free of any dust and debris.

2. Once it's clean, apply a thin layer of PVA glue on to the surface using a brush. If you are intending to cover a large surface area, divide it up into sections and deal with one area at a time. This will prevent the glue from drying prematurely and leave you more time for sculpting. Grab some sheets of tissue roll and start by laying them onto the PVA surface. Ensure the edges slightly overlap so that you are not left with any gaps. If the paper starts tearing as a result of too much PVA glue being applied, add more layers to soak it up.

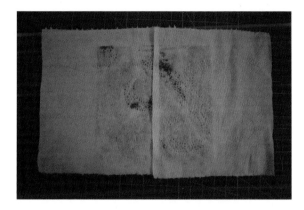

Tissue roll is applied to the base using PVA and an old paintbrush. Any texture or pattern on the tissue roll will quickly disappear in the following steps.

3. Once the area is covered, dip a paintbrush into some more PVA and start stippling the surface. This first pass is more to ensure the tissue roll is firmly stuck down rather than texturing.

An old paintbrush dipped in PVA glue is used to stipple the tissue roll and create texture. Do not worry about any overlap – this can be stippled and blended out.

4. Gradually start to form the waves and ripples. For smaller waves, simple push the brush in one direction slightly as you stipple to form small 'wrinkles' in the tissue roll.

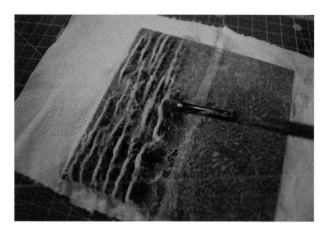

Individual waves are built up by pushing the paintbrush into the tissue roll while it is still wet.

5   Ensure that the motion of the waves is consistent. Be aware of the direction the waves are travelling, how far apart they are from one another and their intensity. The waves will only change direction if they interact with another object.

The effect you are going for will determine the pattern of waves – a calm day will result in a mirror-like surface, while a gale will create defined crests and sea spray. This may potentially require additional materials such as cotton balls.

6. Larger waves can be built up by mixing pieces of tissue with PVA into a thick paste, which can then be applied directly to the surface. Waves can also be formed by

removing tissue. This is especially helpful with larger waves if you've applied too much to the surface.

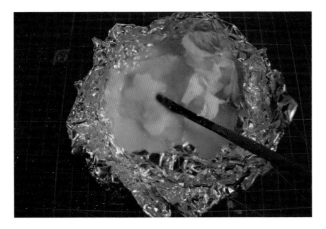

Larger waves can be built up using extra tissue roll soaked in PVA then dolloped onto the surface. If the PVA needs watering down, avoid adding too much water, as the waves will lose definition.

7. It is best to apply larger waves once the smaller ones have been allowed to dry slightly, to reduce the risk of the application removing any detail and definition that is already there. The tacky layer below will also help to fix the second layer of larger waves.

It is best to apply the larger waves once the smaller waves have dried slightly, otherwise any definition in the existing texture could be easily wiped away.

8. Once you are satisfied, leave the surface to dry completely. Resist the urge to tear off the excess tissue – this can be removed with a scalpel without damaging the surface area once dried. The surface can then be painted, varnished and built up with additional texture if desired.

Allow the tissue roll to dry completely before trimming any edges, as the tissue can easily tear when saturated with adhesive.

Note the varying stages of the waves – the crashing breakers in the distance, then the rolling white water before the waves condense down into thin ridges then sink into the sand.

Final water sample.

Rocks: Filler

Scatter can be bought from any number of places, but it can become very expensive when you consider all of the different textures, sizes and colours. If you only have a small area to cover, this becomes even less economical. This technique not only saves you money, but offers an incredibly realistic finish using a medium that can be found in a supermarket!

> **MATERIALS AND EQUIPMENT**
>
> - Filler; often found ready mixed in tubs at DIY stores and supermarkets, it dries from a paste into a solid and can be sanded once so
> - Greaseproof paper on which to spread the filler (do not substitute with tin foil, as the filler will stick to it)
> - Spatula to spread out and smooth the filler
> - Sieve to pass the dried filler through, potentially multiple times
> - Containers – at least two
> - PVA glue, preferably a thicker wood glue
> - Gloves
> - Washes to add definition

Pros

- Accessible – everything listed is a typical household item
- Non-toxic and easy to apply
- Can be mixed with store-bought scenic if desired (your current scatter isn't wasted)
- Can build up larger quantities quite easily if you have the room

Cons

- Covering large areas will require a lot of space for preparation
- As we are essentially making scatter from scratch, it will take more time to create than buying the equivalent quantity from a store

Tips and Tricks

- Mixing together the different results from this technique will create more realistic and natural variation – never use just one size of something.
- You can achieve a realistic finish to this technique with simple acrylic washes.
- If the scale is incorrect, simply put the scatter back through a sieve.
- You can stain and dye your scatter by mixing a small amount of paint in with the filler when wet. You may want separate tubs if creating multiple colours.

Step-by-Step Method

1. Lay out a sheet of greaseproof paper. Using a spatula (or your finger) spread out a layer of ready-mixed filler. The thickness will partially determine the size of your scatter.

Creating rocks for scatter with filler.

2. Allow the filler to dry completely before breaking it up into pieces small enough to place into a sieve. A good technique for this is to roll the greaseproof paper like a roulade.

After leaving the filler to dry, shards are broken off and placed into a sieve. Thinner layers of filler will make this next stage much easier, but it is entirely down to personal preference.

3. Place the filler debris into a sieve and start shaking to separate the large piece of filler from the smaller. You may want to crush pieces with your hand or a utensil to help break them down. Ensure you are sieving into a container so that there is no mess.

The shards of dry filler are rubbed into the sieve to create two different sizes of rock. Any dust or powder that forms will disappear in later stages.

4. You will be left with your small rock scatter in your container, and your larger scatter left behind in the sieve. The larger scatter in the sieve will be slightly rounded as a result of the sieving process, lending itself well to more weathered scenes.

The larger grade of rocks left in the sieve. Notice how the edges are slightly rounded due to being rubbed against the sieve. This is ideal for any water-based scenes or dioramas.

5. The smaller scatter left in the container will also contain a significant amount of powder, as the filler breaks down during the sieving process. This is nothing to worry about as the powder will dissolve into the adhesive when applied to the scene.

The thinner grade of rocks is ideal as ballast, pebbles or general ground cover.

6. The scatter can be stuck to the scene in a number of ways. You can apply glue directly to the surface and sprinkle the scatter on top. The downside to this is that the higher particles will become dislodged later on. Another approach is to apply the scatter and drop diluted PVA to secure it in place (ideal for track ballast). In this example, the rocks are mixed with PVA to create a paste which is then spread over the surface directly.

The filler rocks are mixed with PVA to form a paste which can be spread over any surface. Use less PVA to create a grittier, more defined texture. Use more PVA if a level, smoother surface is desired.

7. Using more PVA will help the mixture to level out. One concern at this stage is to pop any air bubbles that rise to the surface, as these will otherwise leave blemishes when the mixture sets.

In real life, many rock paths are actually fairly flat, with the rocks being pushed into the earth after decades of use. The filler technique helps to replicate this effect.

A lot of PVA was used here, so the mixture levelled out nicely. Any air bubbles should be popped with a cocktail stick to avoid blemishing the final texture.

8. This texture really comes to life after several washes have been applied. Washes will add much-needed definition and depth to the surface that are lacking up until this stage.

Final filler rocks sample.

A black wash reveals the final texture and reintroduces much-needed definition. Ensure the PVA has dried completely before painting otherwise the filler rocks can reactivate, which will result in lost texture.

Ground Cover: Mixed Spices and Materials

It is amazing just how many materials there are around our home that can be used to create stunning miniature effects – even a simple tea bag can create one of the best ground textures. There are so many items in our cupboards that we can use, and nowhere is this truer than when we are creating scenery. This technique of making ground cover uses many familiar items such as herbs, spices, tea leaves, brushes, and even old rags and clothes if desired. It is important to have a little faith with this technique, as it will only start to look satisfying towards the end.

MATERIALS AND EQUIPMENT

- Spray bottle
- PVA glue
- Assorted brushes (maybe a paintbrush, toothbrush and scrubbing brush – all old, as they will be damaged in the process)
- Sponges
- Sieve
- Greaseproof paper to be the base for 'bristle bushes'
- Dried herbs and spices
- Paints (acrylic and/or spray paint, depending on preference) and washes
- Hairspray (optional but good for setting scenes and for shaping long fibre materials)
- Scissors

Pros

- Adds a lot of interest to the scene, as it is overflowing with texture
- Uses readily available materials – most of these can be found in a kitchen
- Your scene will have more natural tones and textures as a by-product of using more natural materials
- A technique you can enjoy smelling!

Cons

- You need to gather a lot of materials together to ideally hit this in one go
- Experimentation is very much advised here, as the final finish can change wildly depending on your choice of materials

Tips and Tricks

- To help form the bushes and grass areas, inflate a balloon and rub it against some clothing to generate static. Pass this over your grass textures to help to lift up the strands.
- Pre-prepare any elements that require dyeing and making in larger batches.
- Combining different herbs and spices will create different textural scatters – experiment with this to replicate your choice of season more accurately.

Step-by-Step Method

1. In your spray bottle, make up your glue mixture out of 50 per cent PVA, 50 per cent water and a small drop of washing-up liquid.
2. Begin by creating scenic material. Use sponges for denser foliage and hedges. Brushes are an easy starting point for making grass. Simply take some scissors and trim the bristles to the required length. Ensure a container is below to collect the fibres. Next, mix the bristles with some acrylic paint until the desired shade is reached, and leave to dry.

Creating ground cover with mixed herbs and materials.

3. The dry materials will tend to clump together, so the next stage is to pass them through a sieve to separate the individual fibre and particles. Depending on how matted the fibres are, you may need to tease them gently apart with your fingers.

The stained fibres are pushed through a sieve, which is the most effective way of breaking up any clumps.

4. Alongside this, start creating some ready-made bushes and grass strips by arranging dots and splodges of PVA glue on a sheet of greaseproof paper. The more irregular the dots are, the more natural and realistic the final effect will be.

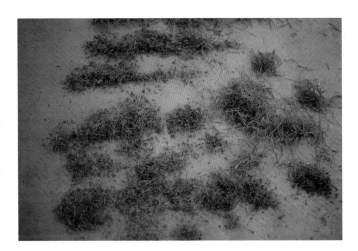

The resulting scatter created from the fibre clumps being passed through the sieve are sieved over the glue dots. Lighter, smaller fibres may need gently pressing into the glue to ensure that they are secured. Once dry, these can be peeled off like stickers and applied to the scene.

5. Sprinkle a selection of your previously made scatter material onto the glue dots and strips. Try not to be too neat with this and resist the urge to interfere as, again, the more random the better. Allow the glue to set, tip the sheet up slightly and collect the spare material for use in a later project.

Glue dots arranged in rows on a sheet of baking paper to create bushes and strips of grass. Try not to be too neat – the more irregularity the better.

6. The ground is prepared by mixing tea leaves with PVA glue and then spreading the mixture out across the desired surface. Pop any air bubbles as they rise to the surface to avoid any unwanted blemishes in the final effect.

An earth texture is built up by mixing tea leaves with PVA. The more PVA, the quicker the mixture will self-level.

7. Mixed herbs and other materials of your choosing can be added once the ground texture has set to create more natural variety.

On top of the dry tea leaf layer, a path is marked out using PVA before mixed herbs and chilli flakes are scattered over to simulate twigs, leaves and natural debris.

8. How the scenic materials are layered will depend entirely on the desired outcome. In this instance, for a dirt track, the materials are layered perpendicular to one another, starting with grass towards the very edges of the track itself and ending with thicker foliage and the hint of wheat fields further away. Secure the scatter in place by dropping diluted PVA over the entire scene with a pipette.

The base is painted to blend the various textures together before the various scatter materials are applied using PVA glue. Do not worry about blending at this point – this stage is purely about getting the material down onto the build.

9. Once the glue has been left to set, washes and dry-brushing techniques can be used to add greater depth of colour and definition to the scene. If any weathering powders have been used, such as in this scene where eyeshadow has been applied to the dirt track, then set them in place with a hairspray or appropriate fixative.

Blending is achieved through washes and dry-brushing. Any shiny areas resulting from the adhesive (unless a wet finish is desired) can be dulled through the application of eyeshadow or weathering powders.

A good image to demonstrate how natural textures are not separate from one another – the scattered leaves help tie in the whole scene.

Final ground cover sample.

Slate Chippings: Eggshell

Slate chippings are a common sight in gardens and parks, offering up beautiful shades of blue and purple. Several of the techniques already discussed would go some way to accurately replicating this texture, but none come as close as broken eggshell.

This technique is a little more time-consuming than others but the results speak for themselves. This method relies heavily on washes and dry-brushing techniques. Washes are needed for depth and contrast whilst dry-brushing is needed to emphasise the crisp edges of the eggshell.

MATERIALS AND EQUIPMENT

- PVA glue
- Eggshell
- Container for breaking up the eggshell and then mixing it with PVA glue into a paste
- Blunt implement – the end of an old paintbrush was used in this example – to crush the eggshell to the desired consistency

---

Pros

- One of the simplest techniques available
- Very cost-effective
- Big batches can be built up quickly and easily
- Surprisingly easy to paint, as washes will soak happily amongst the scatter despite the relatively sharp edges and will do most of the work for you

Cons

- Can be awkward to prepare, given the need to remove the inner lining from the eggshell

Tips and Tricks

- Ensure that the eggshell is as clean as possible before you start crushing it, otherwise an unworkable paste will form in the container when you mix in the glue.

- Mix more PVA than you think you need to help the mixture level out after application.
- Crush the eggshell as much as possible by hand initially to make the grinding stage quicker.
- Pop any air bubbles as they rise to the surface quickly to avoid any blemishes in the final texture.
- An effective way to achieve a greater depth of colour is painting the final texture white and simply colouring with various washes.

Step-by-Step Method

1. Take some empty eggshells and remove the inner lining. This may be difficult to see at first, but can be quickly found by rubbing a finger up and down the inner surface. If the lining is still there, it will ruckle almost instantly and can be peeled off.

Creating slate chippings using eggshell.

2. Break the eggshell up by hand initially before dispensing into a container for grinding.

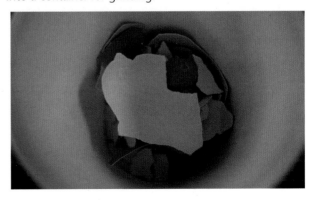

Eggshell is crushed by hand and placed into a container. Ensure that the eggshell has been washed and dried thoroughly before this step.

3. Using a blunt implement, grind the eggshell down until the desired consistency is achieved. Larger pieces of eggshell will tend to sink to the bottom, so sticking in a finger to dislodge them may be necessary at times.

Using a blunt implement, grind the eggshell down into fine particles. Mix the particles up as you go to bring larger chunks back to the surface.

4. Mix the eggshell with PVA glue to form a thick, gritty paste and apply directly to the scene. Air bubbles may rise to the surface as the mixture sets; ensure that these are popped to avoid any blemishes in the final texture.

Mix the eggshell with PVA glue and apply to the surface. Any overhanging particles can be cut or sanded down once the surface has been allowed to dry.

Slate chipping springs up with beautiful hues of blues and purples – it is far from grey.

Final slate chipping sample.

Foliage: Grated Sponge

'Foliage' refers to leaves in general, and can include anything from the smallest of weeds to mighty oak trees. Using sponge to create foliage is incredibly cost-effective and remarkably easy. By gathering different types and colours, a wide range of textural effects can be created.

MATERIALS AND EQUIPMENT

- Sponges; ideally ones with scourers on one side, as this will help hold them together as they're grated
- PVA glue, watered down slightly to ensure that it is thoroughly soaked up by the sponge
- Grater(s) (different sizes will help to create variety)
- Paint (thinned to help it flow through the sponge) and washes
- Gloves
- Dried herbs (optional) to introduce additional texture

Pros

- One of the simplest techniques available
- Very cost-effective, considering the retail price of foliage products
- Big batches can be built up quickly and easily
- Surprisingly easy to paint, as washes will soak happily into the sponge, before or after grating, allowing you to create a real depth of colour and range of tones rarely found in store-bought products

Cons

- This technique can be awkward, as the sponge can resist considerably when pressed against the grater, so patience will be required

Tips and Tricks

- If more tonal variation is needed, grate different coloured sponges into the same mix. When stained, they will carry subtle colour variations, which creates natural variety.
- Roll the sponges tightly as you grate them for more control.
- If you would like to build up more texture, drizzle thinned PVA to apply another layer.
- To create the impression of small flowers, apply paint to a toothbrush or stiff paintbrush and flick paint onto the finished foliage.

Step-by-Step Method

1. Wearing gloves, grate your sponge into a container. Once grated, mix the sponge together with some diluted PVA glue and press into clumps with your hands. Lay down a thick layer of glue to the base and press the sponge into the surface.

Creating foliage using grated sponge.

2. To add textural variety, sprinkle mixed herbs and spices onto the sponge while it is still wet so that the herbs are secured in place. Ignore how wet and soft the surface may be at this stage – when it has been left to dry it will be surprisingly solid.

Atop the grated sponge, mixed herbs are scattered to add textural variety. Any that scatter around the foliage can either be brushed away or left for added texture.

3. Use washes to stain the sponge, building up several layers of colour to ensure thorough coverage. To build up additional texture, sprinkle herbs over the surface again but leave them unpainted this time and spray with a watered-down PVA solution. Flick paint from an old toothbrush to add details such as flowers if desired.

The sponge is coloured using watered-down paints and washes. It is a good idea to blend different colours as you work your way across the foliage to add more natural variety.

4. One difficulty with this technique is accessing the nooks and crannies of the dried sponge. Washes will go quite a way to solving this problem but do not be afraid of taking a paintbrush and being quite forceful with the application of much stronger shades of paint. This will only add depth and contrast to the scene.

Once dry, the areas of the foliage that would be hit directly with light are dry-brushed with a lighter shade to highlight the surface and add depth.

Final foliage sample.

Looking closely at areas of hedgerow reveals there are many different-shaped leaves, which add a great variety of texture. Mixed herbs help to replicate this.

CHAPTER 5

WEATHERING

Weathering defines the reactions that take place all around us between the atmosphere and the environment. These can be reactions within nature itself, or between nature and manufactured materials.

Weathering is crucial to any model (unless you are creating something that's brand new), as it not only bases the model within your scene but also defines things like its age, its condition, what it has been through and so on. This presents a common problem: credibility. Many modellers overdo their weathering in the pursuit of authenticity, often as a result of poor referencing or simply an over-zealous hand. Weathering must be just as accurate as any other element of your scene.

The techniques covered in this chapter cover both common and more case-specific effects, and, more than other chapters, encourage experimentation. When trying out these techniques, it is advisable to practise different strengths. For rust, for example, create a sample with small streaks or stains. Then create another with more pronounced patches, before a final sample where almost the entire surface is the effect itself. This way you can better understand the effect you're going for and compare it more accurately to your image references.

Making Literacy

Weathering is all about balance and reaction. How does rust form, and how much of it would have formed on this particular material, over this period of time, in your chosen climate? Other technical questions to consider include:

Material – Weathering effects interact with different materials in different ways. Rain marks, for instance, would appear differently on glass windows from how they would on exposed metal sheets. This more scientific aspect of your project is where your research should begin.

Time – One of the biggest and most important factors – how long has your material or object been exposed to the elements? Weathering is a great indicator of age and treatment. Also take into account that particularly old models may contain multiple forms of weathering.

Flow – How does your weathering flow around your model? Where would it form and build up? How would it spread? How does it change the material texture as it forms? Are there any colour changes?

Your model – Weathering can be a messy business, so how are you going to protect your model and any elements you do not want affected?

When to Apply Weathering Elements

Weathering is often applied once all of the elements of your model have been brought together. A dust storm, for example, would affect every single thing within your scene, so it is only logical to add appropriate weathering once your model has been composed and painted. Some exceptions apply; for example, with a rusty car in a garage diorama, you would build and finish the elements separately. If you are a prop maker, the weathering stage would come after painting, applying any decals, and sealing with an appropriate form of varnish.

Rust: Cinnamon and PVA

Rust is often a model maker's delight as it introduces a fantastic dose of texture along with a wealth of vivid colours. However, with this comes a downside – it is an exceptionally easy technique to overdo. Image reference is vital, more to rein yourself in rather than to replicate the qualities of the texture itself. Also important to note is that rust differs from corrosion, as it only forms when iron is exposed to oxygen; hence the two separate methods outlined in this chapter.

MATERIALS AND EQUIPMENT

- Cinnamon powder
- PVA glue – watered-down craft PVA, as opposed to a wood glue, to ensure that it dries clear
- Palette knife
- Paint and washes (optional)

Pros

- Quick and easy; very few stages to this technique
- Very few – and easily accessible – materials needed
- Realistic as long as you follow your image reference
- Smells fantastic

Cons

- The colour will be very uniform, so you may wish to introduce some additional shades once dry

- The cinnamon and PVA mixture dries very quickly once mixed, so you have a shorter window to work with this than other techniques

Tips and Tricks

- Using less cinnamon will create a runnier substance that will dry to form a smoother finish, while using more cinnamon will create a much stickier paste that will leave a rougher finish.
- If you wish to introduce more tones once dry, washes will retain the texture. Applying paint directly will ruin the finish.
- Use Blu Tack, or a similar medium, to mask off areas you do not want covered.

Step-by-step Method

1. Mix the cinnamon and PVA glue in equal quantities. Once mixed, add more cinnamon or more PVA depending upon the desired finish.

Creating a rust texture with cinnamon and PVA glue.

2. The mixture will quickly become quite sticky and start to dry as a result of the cinnamon reacting with the PVA. While there is a good amount of working time with this technique, the quicker the paste is applied, the more time it has to level out.

Mix the cinnamon with the PVA in a container. Adding more cinnamon will create a grittier texture, but it will leave you with less working time.

3. Apply the mix to the surface of the model using a palette knife or similar utensil. Once applied, the paste can be easily manipulated with the knife or a cocktail stick.

A lot of PVA had been mixed in with the cinnamon to ensure the mixture levels out well. Apply to the surface using a blunt implement and spread evenly.

4. Ensure that any bubbles that form are quickly popped with a cocktail stick to prevent any blemishes. Once the texture has dried, colour can be built up quite easily. Washes are ideal to add extra tones to the technique. Paint will mask the surface, while washes are thin enough to flow through the grain-like texture. No preparation is needed, as the PVA will have sealed the surface.

Once the area has been left to dry, check for a while after for air bubbles. Pop as many as possible with a cocktail stick or similar to reduce the number of blemishes in the final texture.

These rusty beams are covered in a dense reddish brown, while each face then bears the markings of various weathering processes. Once the cinnamon has dried, additional weathering effects can be applied.

Final rust sample.

Streaking: Pastel Powder and Eyeshadow

There is a huge selection of weathering powders out there for creating oil streaks, rain marks and a wide assortment of dirt and decay. While these are very convenient, the costs can quickly mount up. Not only can this expense be reduced significantly, but your colour options can be greatly expanded, with relative ease. A box of pastels, or even an eyeshadow palette, does exactly the same job as most weathering powders while providing a much wider selection of colours.

MATERIALS AND EQUIPMENT

- Pastels or eyeshadow (avoid anything oil-based, as they will not work for this technique)
- Steel ruler or blunt scalpel for scraping (only if using pastels)
- Soft applicator (such as brush or sponge)
- Setting spray (such as a cheap hairspray, to help to prevent the transfer of powder)

Pros

- Incredibly cheap technique; you will most likely have these materials to hand already
- An enjoyable method that leaves little mess and can be done with minimal set-up
- Instant results – there is no need to wait for anything to dry

Cons

- Pastels may be more complicated to acquire than other materials, but a good newsagents should suffice
- Even with something as common as hairspray, be mindful of your environment; it is always best to wear a mask just to be on the safe side

Tips and Tricks

- If pastel powder or eyeshadow is being applied to a rough surface, use a brush, as a sponge applicator will tear itself apart.
- Varied application techniques create varied results. For example, stippling powders can create impact marks (ideal for bullet holes).
- If an oilier texture is desired, using a damp brush to 'slicken' the surface will make the powder flow as intended.
- Should any debris form, either from sponge disintegrating or from excess powder, blow it away rather than wiping, as this will avoid an unwanted mess.

Step-by-Step Method

1. If using pastels, scrape the sticks using a suitable tool to form a powder. Load up your applicator by simply dipping it into the powder. If using eyeshadow, load up your applicator with just a small amount to begin with. Eyeshadow is usually quite pigmented, so a little goes a long way. Different shades can be mixed if desired.

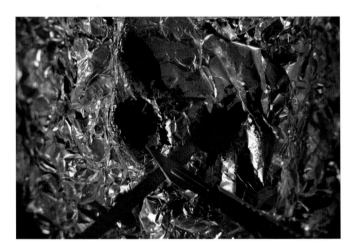

Creating streaking effects with pastels and eyeshadow.

2. Apply to the surface, working in the direction the streaking effect would naturally form in. Use your image references to analyse exactly how the effect would have formed and its strength.

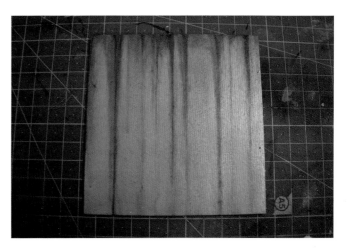

Streaks are initially set down using a make-up applicator for eyeshadow or a brush for pastel. To create wet or fuel streaks, dip a brush into some water and then drag the eyeshadow down across the surface. The damp brush can also be used to blend the streaks out if they are too harsh.

In this example, a multitude of different streaks have been added for effect. In practice, one general colour with some subtle lighter or darker tones would be more appropriate.

Not only are various shades of colour built up in individual streaks, but different tones are also added to each streak itself.

This gate panel, with its iron fence above, is showing the signs of many rainfalls, with rust running down the surface.

3. Once satisfied, apply a layer of fixing spray to ensure the surface cannot be disturbed. If the model is not going to be handled, this step could be omitted; however, it will make cleaning the model easier in future and is simply good practice.

Final streaking sample.

Corrosion: Salt and Water

By applying a layer of salt on top of a painted surface and then applying a second coat of paint, the salt effectively forms a mask that can then be chipped away to expose the first layer. This technique balances control with a natural aesthetic randomness: you are in charge of where the salt is applied, but the actual scattering of the salt crystals will lead to a more natural effect. This is one of the most technical techniques in this book, and some experimentation will be required to achieve the desired finish.

MATERIALS AND EQUIPMENT

- Salt, ideally in a mix of crystal sizes
- Water
- Two containers for the salt and water
- Paintbrush (or airbrush if you have one)
- Toothbrush with stiff bristles to chip away the salt at the end
- Paint in two different colours for the base layer and top layer
- Kitchen roll, sponges or cotton buds to clean up any excess water and to move the salt around if desired

---

Pros

- A natural finish often improved by mistakes – the less control, the better
- A safe and clean technique
- The materials used will last a long time, incurring little expense
- Drying times can be used to continue with other elements of the project

Cons

- Experimentation is needed to achieve the desired finish
- Drying times can mount up, especially in colder weather, so be aware of this if a deadline looms
- Applying decals on top of this texture can be difficult. Setting mediums will make this easier but, again, experimentation is essential

Tips and Tricks

- Place the model on a turntable or a surface that is easy to manoeuvre to avoid any risk of disturbing the surface when drying.
- Have everything to hand when starting this technique. Anything that minimises movement while creating the texture will be beneficial.
- Achieve a more varied and natural look with different types of salt. It is a good idea to use both rock salt and table salt, as mixing the grain sizes will give more texture and a more varied and natural look.
- Choose a salt crystal size appropriate to the scale of the model being made.
- Do not be concerned about any salt that becomes dislodged – it is incredibly difficult to spoil this effect.

Step-by-Step Method

1. Ensure the model is clean and free of dust. Fill a container with water and another with salt. Check that the work space is clear of anything that could be knocked over and create a mess.

Creating corrosion with salt and water.

2. Apply a layer of paint. This needs to be the colour of the exposed material, so in effect this technique works backwards – the most recent colour is applied last. An airbrush is perfect for this technique, but a paintbrush and a steady hand will suffice.

An initial layer of rust is applied as a base. A simple mix of oranges, reds and browns are stippled onto the surface. Even stippling will add a small amount of texture that will make a noticeable different in the final texture.

Salt crystals are sprinkled over the wet areas. Mixing two different sizes of salt crystal will create more natural rough edges and add variety.

3. Once the first layer of paint is dry, apply water to areas where corrosion will form. Try not to add too much water at once or it will run all over the model and make creating specific textured areas difficult.

5. Allow the water and salt to dry completely. The salt will return to a much brighter white when dry.

Water is applied to the surface in areas where rust is to show through in the final product. Apply more water than is needed, as the final amount of rust showing through will be smaller than this area.

Allow the water to dry completely before moving on to the next step. If there is any trace of water, the salt will simply brush off in the next step, which is exactly what we want to avoid. Instead, we want the water to dry completely so that the salt is lightly glued to the surface.

4. Sprinkle salt onto areas covered with water. When the water dries, this will 'glue' the salt to the surface to form a mask. A lot of salt will fall off the model while it is being applied, so persevere until the desired coverage is achieved.

6. Apply a second layer of paint all over the surface of the model. This will be a different colour from the first layer, and is often the paint that has been applied to the under-lying material, for example painted metal sheets. If using an airbrush, spray from a distance, as the air can dislodge the salt; if using a brush, be very gentle to avoid the same

problem. Do not worry too much, however – a few crystals becoming dislodged is inevitable.

A thin layer of acrylic paint is stippled on using a paintbrush. An airbrush will achieve more realistic results but a traditional paintbrush will also work. Leave the paint to dry completely. This layer of paint is the colour that the material was when it was new.

7. Once the second layer of paint has dried, take a wet paintbrush and start chipping off the salt. Do not be afraid to use a bit of force for this, as the second layer of paint will be helping to hold the salt down a little.

Once the paint has dried, take a soft paintbrush and soak it in water. Gently start rubbing the wet brush over the areas where salt has been applied. Using a stiff brush will scratch the surface of the paint and dislodge too much material.

8. When the salt has been removed, there should be patches exposing the first layer of colour. Sometimes leaving small areas of salt on your model, especially in gaps and recesses, can be a great way of creating additional weathering.

As the wet brush dampens the top layer of paint, the salt will start to chip away, revealing the rust layer below. The amount of rust showing through is initially determined by how much salt has been applied, but a more vigorous rubbing of the paintbrush over the surface will start to chip away more of the paint.

This shipping container was once entirely bright blue before the salty air started to take effect. In this instance, the chipping is actually exposing an older coat of paint. If more layers are desired, simply apply more sheets of paint prior to the application of salt and water.

Final corrosion sample.

Moss: Mixed Herbs and Cinnamon

This technique follows on nicely from others already covered in this book, as it combines several different materials used so far. Moss is very similar to rust and corrosion in that it grows in patches and forms such wonderful texture, as though consuming the material it has formed on. With moss, it is very important to consider scale – it may be the case that the scale is so small that a simple wash will suffice.

MATERIALS AND EQUIPMENT

- Mixed dried herbs – the more varied, the better
- Cinnamon
- PVA glue
- Container for the glue mixture
- Spatula
- Sandpaper
- Paint, watered down to create a wash

Pros

- The materials in this example can be used for other techniques in this book
- The combination of materials creates an incredibly satisfying and varied look
- A diverse technique composed of multiple layers which can be altered and switched around according to the desired texture
- The materials listed are just examples of what could be used for this technique – experiment and explore!

Cons

- Long drying times, as the paste for this method needs to be quite thick
- To aid the paste layer to adhere to the surface, it is best to lay it flat. This may be difficult for certain models. A thicker PVA may help.

Tips and Tricks

- This is one technique where the more mess you create the better, as it will lead to a more natural and realistic finish.
- Applying washes on top of the final paste mixture, once set, will create greater depth and richness of colour.
- If drying times become an issue, especially in colder weather, use a heat gun or hairdryer from a safe distance.

Step-by-Step Method

1. Start by applying a layer of sandpaper onto the desired surface. This will add an initial layer of texture and provide extra grip for the herb paste. Do not worry if the surface the sandpaper is applied to is not flat and creases form – the majority of these will be hidden by the paste.

Creating a moss texture with mixed herbs and cinnamon.

2. Mix several different herbs with PVA in a container. Add some cinnamon to thicken the paste and bind the ingredients together. Do not worry about the colour, as this can be changed as desired later.

A paste is mixed up using mixed herbs, cinnamon and PVA glue. The less PVA glue used the better, as this technique needs the texture of the herbs to shine through as much as possible.

3. Apply the paste to the intended surface using a spatula or, if you have no problem with getting messy, just a finger; the latter helps to smear the paste into the sandpaper and form a solid layer. Although this approach will smooth the surface, it can be roughened up again afterwards with any suitable tool.

As the paste should be quite thick, the easiest method of application is to simply spread it across the surface with a finger. The underlying sandpaper will help to introduce texture in any thinner areas and also help the herb paste stick to the surface.

4. Once the paste has been applied, additional herbs can be added for a looser, thicker texture, or the surface can be manipulated with a suitable implement to make it more uneven. Leave it to dry completely before attempting to paint.

Once an even layer has been created, an old paintbrush can be used to make impressions or alter the surface as needed. It is advisable to neaten up any edges before the paste dries just for ease.

This tree stump has been completely covered in moss, creating a thick carpet of texture. Notice all of the individual colours – these can be stippled and mixed directly onto the surface once the herb paste has dried.

Final moss sample.

Tree Roots: Wire and Glue Gun

Anything organic and natural, such as trees, often causes much hesitation and concern in model makers. In fact, there is very little that can go wrong, as long as the texture of the scenic element being created is understood. Tree roots are a great way of binding the elements of a scene together and can be formed with very little effort. There are many kits out there for trees and similar objects, but they are often very expensive and do not contain enough to cover the planned surface area. This technique, which uses a glue gun to sculpt rather than stick, will help to solve that.

MATERIALS AND EQUIPMENT

- Wire, for example garden wire, to form the 'skeleton' of the tree root and the base of the tree itself; use thicker wire for larger-scale work or wrap multiple smaller strands together
- Glue gun
- Filler to add extra texture at the end
- Paintbrush for stippling
- Gloves
- Wire cutters (scissors will rarely cut through metal)

Pros

- The wire and glue gun can be used quite flexibly, so there is no need to worry about creating a specific shape
- Can be combined with many of the other techniques in this book to add additional texture and to blend the roots into the scene
- Very little drying time, as the glue dries so quickly

Cons

- Ideal for small scales, but for larger models an alternative technique may work better
- Suitable wire and a glue gun may be more difficult to acquire, although glue guns can be found in most hobby stores and wire can be anything. A garden wire is perfect and can be found in DIY shops

Tips and Tricks

- Make long strips of tree root and then cut to size. This makes it simpler and quicker to cover larger surface areas.
- Hold the wire vertically when applying the glue as any drips will run down the wire itself.
- If working on a large scale, try bulking out the wire with tin foil before applying the glue.
- Use a piece of kitchen towel to quickly wipe away any glue that builds up on the glue gun.

Step-by-Step Method

1. Take a length of wire and cut to size. If larger roots are desired, take multiple lengths and twist to form a thicker cable.

Creating tree roots using wire and hot glue.

2. Take the glue gun and start piping hot glue onto the wire. Try not to cover the whole area or apply too much hot glue at once, as it dries incredibly quickly; this enables it to be built up in several layers.

Hot glue is applied to twisted wire to start bulking out the general form of the tree roots. To prevent any notable drips of glue forming, twizzle the wire between your fingers until it has set to keep it evenly spread.

3. Once the glue is dry, rub the hot end of the glue gun back and forth across the surface. This will be hot enough to melt just the surface and will create a satisfying bark texture. Any mistakes can be rectified by applying more hot glue to the areas concerned.

Once the main root system has been established, secure it to the base of your build. Remember to include the shallower roots of other trees that are more buried into the earth – not all roots are perfectly laid out across the surface.

4. Once the desired root system has been created, take some ready-mixed filler and start smearing it around the roots. Decide which roots will dive into the ground and which are more exposed simply by how much filler is covering them. Stipple with a paintbrush to create additional texture. Leave to dry before painting.

To sink the roots into the scene more realistically, take some ready-mixed filler and stipple it around the roots using an old paintbrush. Try to add variety by completely covering some areas of the roots whilst leaving other areas largely exposed.

It can be tempting with elements such as trees to create perfect, curved organic forms, but this does not reflect real life. In this image, the roots form almost 90-degree angles as they work their way across the surface.

Final roots sample.

CHAPTER 6

ARCHITECTURE

Almost all model makers will acquaint themselves with architectural elements at some point, whether that be full-scale architectural builds or a simple stone wall forming part of a larger diorama. Architectural model making can be found in railway modelling, wargaming, professional projects and more.

When it comes to modelling architectural elements, it is important to be aware that no one 'knows' exactly what brickwork, for example, looks like, though they see it every day. Many a student has dived straight in without image references and created a sub-standard outcome because of this. Although architectural materials are a part of our daily lives, they are just as important to research as any other surface.

This chapter looks at five techniques for creating common architectural surfaces. Most surfaces will be weathered to some degree in reality, but the focus here will be purely on the materials themselves. Techniques from Chapter 5 can be used as necessary.

Making Literacy

When it comes to architecture, it is important to understand how construction materials interact with the wider world. Scenery and weathering moulds to the surfaces of buildings and structures, pulling them into the landscape and possibly swallowing them whole. If an 'as new' finish is desired, this requires little thought, but any form of age needs careful planning to not only ensure that it is accurate, but also to prevent excess.

Construction This is the first and most obvious thing to consider. How has the surface been constructed? What techniques could be used in real life? These methods should, to some degree, be mirrored in the miniature replica.

Colour It is easy to assume that many architectural materials are just one colour, but there may actually be many subtle variations that can make or break the final finish. Bricks, for example, contain hundreds of different hues, and even the mortar is not just one colour.

Forces Again, we need to account for whatever forces have been exerted on a structure. High winds will lead to cracks and chipping. Abandonment will lead to foliage gradually consuming the object back into the environment. Explosive projectiles will leave burns and marks on the surface. An understanding of the material and how it reacts to external forces is essential in these instances.

Your model How will you communicate information? If making a building, what environmental elements will you include to explain the level of decay and weathering? Also think practically – tall structures require additional support. Have you constructed a sturdy base, and how well is the model attached to it?

When to Apply Architectural Elements

Anything architectural should be built first. If it is an exterior diorama, then create a very basic general terrain before planting the finished building on top. If it is an interior, construct the basic architectural elements, including walls and floors, first. This is because scenery, weathering and props will all come in later, and will respond to the architecture they are interacting with: scenery will grow around a building, weathering will accumulate on its surface over time, and props will be positioned according to structural boundaries. This approach will help achieve tiny, convincing details such as scratches on the floor from dragged furniture.

GENERAL POINTS TO CONSIDER

- Consider building in sections. Keep walls separate for as long as possible to assist with access.
- If large areas of material are needed, for example brickwork, this can be time-consuming. Consider moulding and casting techniques or any other quicker methods.
- Think about usage. How has a room or building been used? If so, what evidence would that leave? The decisions you make in this regard can elevate the quality of the final model tenfold.

Stone Wall: Egg Carton

This technique requires a little bit of give and take, but the amount of texture that comes through is surprising. The interior of an egg carton has a fantastic rough surface, which, combined with its thickness, makes for great stonework. Carton can be difficult to work with, requiring flattening into an irregular sheet before cutting; this is a very accessible material, however, and a little patience will go a long way.

MATERIALS AND EQUIPMENT

- Cardboard egg carton
- Wood glue (adheres the carton material much better than PVA)
- Scalpel with a new, sharp blade; the cardboard has a tendency to fluff up when cut with a blunt blade
- Steel ruler
- Sandpaper

Pros

- Very accessible material
- No additional texture needed

- When layered, this technique adds a lot of strength to a build
- Great for washes and dry-brushing

Cons

- Slightly awkward material to work with
- Scaling can be tricky, so determine the correct block size before adopting this technique

Tips and Tricks

- Press a steel ruler down on the carton as hard as possible to flatten out the material and to prevent curved edges.
- The 'egg section' is typically more textured than the lid – mix bricks from both for more variety.
- Seal the surface with a thin layer of PVA to assist with painting and washes.
- Use an empty biro pen to round off any corners and crisp edges for a more weathered effect.

Step-by-Step Method

1. Sand the surface onto which the stones will be glued to provide extra adhesion. Paint it black to ensure that no white gaps show through the final texture.

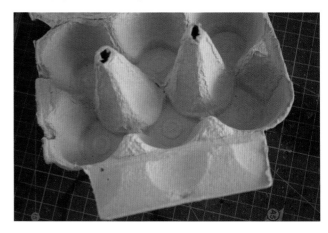

Creating a stone texture with an egg carton.

2. Take a clean egg carton and flatten it out as much as possible. The material will naturally tear due to its irregular shape, but the flipside to this is that there will be more

natural variation. Using a steel ruler and scalpel, start slicing the egg carton into strips from which individual blocks can be cut. Put as much weight behind the steel ruler as possible to keep the edges nice and straight.

Tear up the egg carton into workable chunks that can be laid out as flat as possible. This will be very patchy but will create enough workable material.

3. When enough blocks have been cut out, jumble them up to create more natural variation. Do not worry about any that seem too textured or have irregular formations on the surface – this will all add to the final finish. Even with brick-work, try not to be too controlling of the final outcome.

Cut the egg carton up into tiles that match the working scale. A scalpel is ideal for this, as it will neatly cut through the fibrous material. Scissors should be avoided as they will create a furry edge.

4. Glue rows of blocks down one on top of the other. Think carefully about individual construction techniques, and also be aware of lines becoming more angled as you move up the surface. Draw guidelines with a pencil if necessary.

Glue the tiles down using either a wood glue or a superglue. Mortar should be added for extra realism, but this sample has been made with speed in mind. If mortar is not being added then washes are a must.

The uneven surface of the stones in this image shows how the egg carton is an ideal material for reproducing this. With the addition of ready-mixed filler to imitate the mortar, this image could be replicated exactly.

Final stone brick sample.

Wood Planks: Cardboard and Glue Stick

The number of ways a wood texture can be replicated in miniature could fill a book within itself. Almost any material can be used – styrene, foamboard, paper, paint and of course wood itself. This technique looks at using two common household materials – cardboard and a glue stick. When layered, a glue stick can create a wonderful texture that can just as easily be applied to curved surfaces as flat, meaning this technique can be moulded to virtually any form.

MATERIALS AND EQUIPMENT

- Card; a cereal box is ideal for this technique, although almost any card can be used. Avoid cardboard if possible, as ridges will appear when the glue stick is pressed into the surface
- Glue stick, the older the better. Glue sticks that have partially dried out or leave lumps on the surface are the bane of many a sketchbook, but for this technique they can work wonders
- Glue – if using card that has been printed on one side, use superglue as this will create a strong bond and will add strength to the surface. If not, ideally use a wood glue in thin layers
- Pen
- Scalpel with a new, sharp blade
- Paint – black for the base and whatever colour is desired for the planks

---

Pros

- Incredibly cheap
- Very realistic finish that can be scaled
- Very quick to create in large batches
- More environmentally friendly when using an eco glue stick

Cons

- The card is prone to warping if too much glue is applied
- The glue needs to cure fully prior to painting otherwise it will simply lift off

Tips and Tricks

- Build up several layers of glue for more texture; too many layers, however, and the glue will just fill itself in.
- Etch extra details into the glue as it dries with a cocktail stick or similar implement. More layers will add greater definition and depth.
- Water the paint down slightly to prevent it from filling in the texture.

Step-by-Step Method

1. Start by determining the surface area that needs to be covered and planning out exactly what pattern needs to be made. Paint the surface onto which the planks will be glued black to hide any gaps.

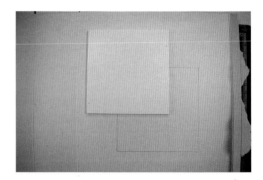

Creating wood planks with card and a glue stick.

2. Draw out the desired number of planks on a piece of card. Include some additional planks that are much longer than needed to fill in any gaps or uneven edges.

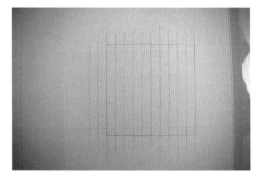

Individual wood planks are marked out on cereal box card. Arrange and cut out as many as possible in one go to avoid uneven edges or scalpel marks.

3. Rub a glue stick back and forth on the card, going in the direction of the planks as drawn. Allow the glue to go slightly tacky between coats to build up a rougher texture, or continually apply glue for a smoother finish.

Creating wood planks with card and a glue stick.

This technique is not reserved for flooring. Wood fences are fairly common sights in model making and this technique could be used to equal effect here.

4. Allow the glue to dry and cure before cutting out the individual planks using a scalpel. Mix the planks up, either by shuffling them on the work surface or by shaking in a bag. This will lead to a more natural finish. Glue the planks down one by one, keeping an eye on pattern and straight edges as you would with brickwork. Place a book or similarly weighted object on top to prevent warping and allow to dry fully before painting.

Final wood plank sample.

Once the planks have been arranged, paint them individually before applying various coats of washes and dry-brushing. Any overreaching planks can be trimmed later, especially if the edges are being covered with details such as skirting boards or wall panelling.

Corrugated Metal: Tin Foil

Corrugated sheeting can be bought pre-moulded from a range of retailers, but it can easily be made from scratch in greater volume for a fraction of the price. While this technique focuses on corrugated metal, it could in fact be applied to any similar corrugated material, for example roof tiles. Additional care must be taken with this technique, as the tin foil is easy to damage while it is being formed; templates can be made to mitigate this issue.

MATERIALS AND EQUIPMENT

- Tin foil (the thicker the better, as it will retain its shape)
- Card to make templates
- Cocktail sticks for the templates
- Paintbrush or toothbrush to help press the tin foil into the template
- Superglue
- Glue gun
- Black paint

Pros

- A roll of tin foil will last for a long time if used solely for model making
- Very easy to scale
- Lightweight – no worries with regards to structural integrity
- Much cheaper than pre-formed alternatives

Cons

- Very easy to damage – care must be taken when handling the finished product
- Can be difficult to glue, as tin foil does not like many adhesives

Tips and Tricks

- Fold the tin foil in half before cutting to create extra thickness and rigidity.
- Use a toothbrush or similar tool to press the tin foil gently down into the first template, otherwise there is a risk the foil could tear prior to clamping.
- Ensure that the tin foil is smooth before you press the templates together, as any creases will be noticeable in the final finish.
- If smooth edges are desired, fold them over before clamping. This will add some convincing thickness to the end while hiding the rough edge when glued.

Step-by-Step Method

1. Start by painting the surface to which the tin foil will be applied with a black paint. Although the entire area may be covered, this texture will be quite three-dimensional and it may be possible to look under the material.

Creating corrugated metal using tin foil.

2. Take a sheet of tin foil and fold in half to add extra strength. This sheet needs to be slightly larger than the intended surface, as the final panels will overlap. Cut out panels, alternating the size slightly for each.

A sheet of tin foil is cut out and folded in half to add extra strength. Panels of the correct size and scale are cut out using a scalpel and steel ruler. Creases should not necessarily be avoided as, depending on the level of weathering, these can simulate extensive damage.

3. Take a piece of scrap material and glue cocktail sticks evenly spaced along one face. Create two of these templates.

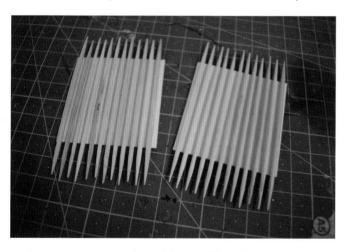

Two templates are created for moulding the tin foil into corrugated sheets. Cocktail sticks are superglued to a piece of scrap material, with an equal gap left in between each one.

4. Take a piece of tin foil and gently press it into the surface of one of the templates using a paintbrush, toothbrush or just a finger.

The second template is added on top of the tin foil and the two are squeezed together. Avoid exerting too much pressure, as either the tin foil or the templates could break.

5. Place the second template onto the tin foil and press the templates together so the foil creases. Then gently prise them apart and lift off the corrugated material.

A piece of tin foil is pressed into one of the templates to hold it in place. This technique actually works perfectly well just by doing this, but the use of two templates does create more definition.

6. It is best to lay the panels directly onto the work surface instead of a container; the action of taking them out of the container may lead to damage, as the tin foil is so delicate. Handling the foil with tweezers may be necessary.

Gently remove the tin foil from the templates, being careful not to press any of the detail out. Repeat until the desired amount have been created.

7. Very gently place the individual panels onto the desired surface, using small blobs of hot glue to stick them in place. Tackle each panel individually, as hot glue dries quickly and force should be avoided with this technique.

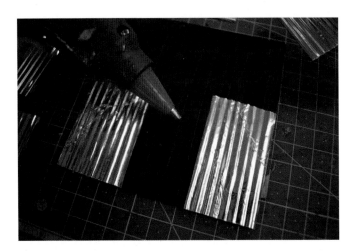

Various different adhesives could work in the application of the corrugated panels to the base, but hot glue has the added bonus of filling in any undesirable gaps. Care needs to be taken in ensuring that the glue does not dry too quickly and that in the process of pressing the tin foil down, detail is not damaged and lost.

8. If any edges start to curl up, or if the layers of tin foil start to separate, add extra hot glue where needed. In practice, these can also be left, as the paintwork will likely be sufficient to glue down any loose edges.

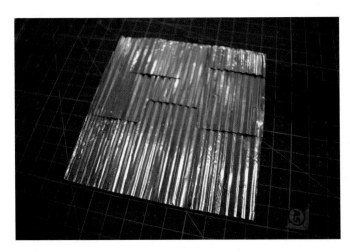

Layer the panels up as desired. Any rough or folded edges can be quickly moved back into place and secured using tweezers.

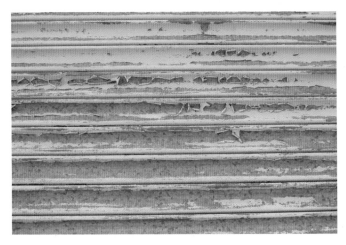

Corrugated metal can be surprisingly beautiful when the paint starts to peel along the upper surfaces.

Final corrugated metal sample.

Concrete: Filler

Often this texture is simply painted onto a flat surface which leaves a flat and far from inspiring finish. This is probably because concrete is perceived as a fairly uninteresting material that requires little attention to pull off, but that is far from the case. Concrete can have an amazing wealth of colour and an almost marble-esque network of veins. Externally, concrete can be covered in all sorts of cracks and indentations, and incorporating these elements into a build will yield much more impressive results.

MATERIALS AND EQUIPMENT

- Filler, ideally ready-mixed to avoid any further preparatory steps
- Sandpaper
- Spatula (optional) for neater application of the filler
- Black paint
- PVA glue to seal

Pros

- Very few materials needed
- Very easy to apply and natural results
- Large areas can be covered very quickly
- The filler can be used to blend other elements of the build into the surface

Cons

- Thicker layers can take a long time to dry
- The final finish cannot be controlled, so trial and error is the rule of the day

Tips and Tricks

- If the surface that is to be covered in filler is smooth, roughen it with sandpaper in at least two different directions for greater adhesion.

- Extra details can be scratched into the surface of the filler both before and after it has dried.
- Apply a thinned layer of PVA gently onto the surface of the filler once dry to seal the surface for painting.
- If certain areas of the filler are too sharp when dry, take a wet paintbrush and gently rub it over the section in question. This will round out any protruding material.

Step-by-Step Method

1. Paint the surface area black. This step is not actually essential, but it does make seeing the texture as it is applied much clearer.

Creating a concrete texture using filler.

2. Apply a small amount of filler to the intended surface, spreading it around with an implement or a finger. No texture needs to be added at this point – it is simply about getting the filler down.

Smear some ready-mixed filler across the surface. A brush or palette knife can be used for this, but a finger is much quicker and easier.

3. Ideally using a finger (but a paintbrush will suffice), stipple the surface of the filler. A small amount of stippling will create small peaks in the surface, which will create a less textured finish, while a large amount of stippling may remove areas of filler and create a much stronger texture. Leave to dry completely.

Using a finger, stipple the surface of the filler whilst it is still wet. Stippling will result in an uneven surface that will create more detail and textural variation during the sanding stage.

4. Once dry, take a sheet of sandpaper and sand the surface back until the texture is as desired. Once this point has been reached, take some wet and dry paper and smooth out any sandpaper scratches. Seal with PVA.

Once the filler has completely dried, take some sandpaper and reduce the texture back to the desired level. A light sanding will leave a lot of texture resulting in a more damaged and weathered finish, whilst more sanding will create a smoother, newer impression. Remember to work through the different grades to remove as many scratches as possible.

There is a wide range of marks to be found in concrete. In this example, leaving some scratches from the sandpaper would actually be desirable as they would imitate the horizontal marks that can be seen mostly in the bottom half of the image.

Final concrete sample.

Brickwork: Card and Filler

Brickwork is a very common texture that most beginner model makers believe is impossible to create without incredible effort. There are in fact many time-saving and cost-effective techniques to achieve good results, although each has its limitations. When it comes to brickwork, scale is everything, as it will determine what level of texture to aim for and the sheer amount of time it will take to create. The method described here works for small to medium-scale builds, and is ideal if custom patterns are intended.

MATERIALS AND EQUIPMENT

- Card, ideally a thin card such as a cereal box
- Filler for the mortar
- Sponge
- Pencil
- Scalpel
- Cocktail stick
- Glue (superglue if using card with a printed side, wood glue/PVA for anything else)

Pros

- No preparation needed – apply straight to the surface
- Ideal for custom brickwork or moulding around corners
- There is some leeway with regards to scale
- Separate areas can be worked on simultaneously

Cons

- Can take a substantial amount of time to cover large areas
- Risk of warping if applied to a porous surface

Tips and Tricks

- Coating the finished brickwork with a thin layer of PVA prior to applying the filler will make clean-up much easier.
- Use a sponge to stipple paint to create more texture on the cardboard surface.

- For custom brickwork, draw the pattern onto the surface of the model to act as a guide. Do not freestyle.
- Use a template, such as a piece of cardboard or plastic, to create the same-sized gap between the bricks as they are placed.

Step-by-Step Method

1. Take a piece of card and start drawing out bricks to the desired scale. Use a pencil where possible, as biro tends to show through paintwork. A biro has been used here simply to make the image clearer.

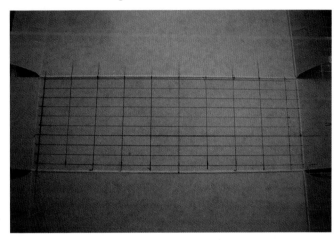

Creating brickwork using card and filler.

2. Cut out the bricks using a scalpel and jumble them up to add more variety.

Bricks are drawn out to scale on a sheet of card and cut out using a scalpel. Jumble them up once complete to add a little natural variation to the final texture.

3. Glue the bricks to the base material. It is essential with brickwork to create straight lines, so mark out some guidelines if needed. For custom brickwork, mark out the general pattern before any application. Make sure to leave a gap between the bricks for mortar.

Guidelines are marked on the surface with pencil to ensure straight lines before the bricks are secured in place using superglue. Wood glue would give a little more working time but superglue was used to seal the edges of the card to prevent fraying and damage. A gap is left between the bricks to leave room for mortar.

4. Smear some filler across the surface. Try not to add too much in one go, as whatever is remaining on the surface will be removed anyway. Use a piece of card to help distribute it evenly.

Ready-mixed filler is spread between the bricks using a scrap piece of card. Apply a decent amount of pressure whilst doing this to ensure that no cavities are left between the bricks.

5. Scrape the surface with a sheet of card to remove as much of the surface filler as possible. This will create almost a perfectly smooth surface, which will be rectified in the next step.

As much filler as possible should be scraped off the surface of the bricks otherwise definition will be lost in the final stages. A good guide to when to stop is when debris starts to form as the exposed faces of the card bricks begin to breakdown.

6. With a slightly damp sponge, wipe away the filler, leaving only that which has been pressed into the gaps between the bricks. This will also remove a small amount of filler from those gaps to bring back some definition to the brickwork.

Wipe a damp sponge over the surface of the bricks while the filler is still wet. This will remove any remaining filler from the surface of the brickwork as well as a smaller amount of filler from the mortar gaps to add greater definition to the bricks themselves.

7. If there is any stubborn filler remaining on the surface of the bricks, dab the sponge over the surface to blend any streaks into the bricks.

Continuing with the damp brush, stipple the surface to lift up some of the card fibres and add a little more roughness to the surface. This will add a bit of texture in the final painting stages.

8. Once the filler has completely dried, take a cocktail stick and etch lines into the mortar if any extra definition is required.

This step is not always necessary, but dragging a cocktail stick along the mortar lines will add an extra level of definition to the brickwork.

Mortar is always slightly recessed into the brickwork and is not always perfectly neat. Tool marks and excess build-up are quite common.

Final brickwork sample.

CHAPTER 7

INTERIORS

When it comes to model-making interiors, there are a great number of things to think about. With scenic elements, relinquishing control and embracing natural chaos is key, while with interiors the exact opposite applies. Interior modelling needs to be measured, precise and controlled, with significant attention directed to how surfaces will be constructed and how they will work alongside the existing architecture. An awareness of core design principles, period, style and colour will also be needed for any interior build. Subsequently, collecting reference images is especially important to ensure authenticity and period accuracy.

This chapter looks at five techniques for creating common interior surfaces. With regards to weathering, everything will be determined by how much use the space gets. A wood plank floor will look much older and scuffed if it has been walked over for many years, for example. Therefore, when looking at the techniques described here, it is important to be aware that they demonstrate just one approach, and different levels of weathering will drastically alter the final finish.

Making Literacy

With interiors, the texture is determined by the finish, which itself is determined by use of the space. Essentially, one of the first things a maker needs to create is a story for what they intend to build, as it will influence a great many elements. A new carpet will build up stains and marks in the hallway or stairs of a family home if left for years on end. Establishing this story changes the paintwork, texturing and maybe even how the initial texture is laid down. Some other thoughts include:

Construction – The most obvious example of this would be a wood plank floor. How have the planks been arranged? How will they mould to the existing room shape? How do they meet up with the base of the walls? Do they spread out evenly across the space?

Colour – As with almost every texture explored so far, colour variation is key in interiors. How many colours are there in wooden furniture? If walls are scuffed and damaged, how many layers of colour are there below? Have walls been painted perfectly or are they slightly mottled?

Forces – Do not be tricked into thinking that the elements have no influence on interiors. Is there any mould, or, even worse, leaks? If so, what marks would be formed? Is wallpaper peeling off? Are there any cracks in the walls or weeds growing around door frames? Are windows perfectly clean?

Your model – Remember to use every tool at your disposal to tell a story. How is furniture arranged? What marks would be made from the furniture moving around? How do people move through the space? How would that change the textures? How are cushions laid out? Where would props be placed?

When to Apply Interior Elements

The architectural elements need to be built first, as these will form the boundaries within which the interior elements will be constructed. However, access can very quickly become an issue here, so it may be wise to keep walls and floors separate to some degree to assist with the painting process in particular.

After this, it is best to think of the interior in layers. Should we build the walls first? Well, is there wall panelling? Yes, so maybe build the floors first so that the panelling can sit over the edge of the floor and create a neater finish. Are there ceiling mouldings? Yes, so paint the walls first and then apply the mouldings separately afterwards, again to create a neater finish. Washes tend not to appear much in interiors so these cannot be relied upon to neaten up any messy paintwork.

GENERAL POINTS TO CONSIDER

- One option could be to build modules that can be painted separately and then arranged later, similar to a doll's house.
- Give thought to the order in which everything will be built – a lot of time and effort can be saved just by writing down a plan.
- Consider use of the room in every detail, as this will influence texture, weathering, arrangement of the space and much, much more.

Leather: Tin Foil

This technique does require a delicate touch. An amazing amount of texture can be gained from a scrunched-up piece of tin foil, but it is incredibly easy to tear while working with it. However, with some care and precision, this technique offers a brilliantly realistic finish that can be moulded to virtually any surface.

MATERIALS AND EQUIPMENT

- Tin foil, the thicker the better to prevent tearing
- Adhesive – what type depends on the surface that the tin foil is being applied to; Wood glue, superglue, double-sided tape will all work on the foil

---

Pros

- Incredibly cheap technique, as one small roll of tin foil will cover a huge area
- No tools required
- A very quick technique, as the initial texture is formed almost instantly
- Can be moulded to any surface – any creases will add to the final effect

Cons

- Tin foil is very easy to rip, so care is needed
- The texturing process means there is very little control over scale

Tips and Tricks

- Fold the tin foil in half after it has been textured to give it some additional strength or to hide any unwanted blemishes on the surface being covered.
- Do not use a glue gun – when the glue dries it will form a solid bead that will be very visible once painted.
- If you do not like how the effect is looking, in most cases you can simply tear off the tin foil and apply a new piece.
- Slightly mould a small area of the tin foil to the object before gluing to help it stay in place as you work on the rest.

Step-by-Step Method

1. Tear off a piece of tin foil slightly larger than the area that needs to be covered and scrunch it into a ball. The tighter it is scrunched, the more texture will be created and the smaller the scale will be.

Creating a leather texture with tin foil.

2. Gently unfold the scrunched-up ball of tin foil, taking as much care as possible to avoid any tears. Once it's unfolded, smooth the tin foil down with your hand to create a flat sheet.

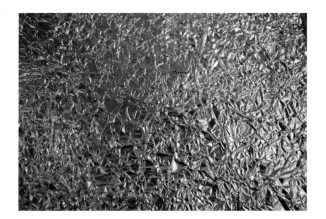

Tin foil is scrunched up and then folded back out. The tin foil should be laid out as flat as possible to determine how much usable material there is.

3. Drag the back of a fingernail across the surface of the tin foil backwards, not forwards. Dragging forwards will instantly tear the foil, while going backwards will smooth out the creases and leave a subtle texture suitable for imitating leather. Do this across the whole surface.

Rub the surface of the tin foil with the back of a fingernail, smoothing out the larger creases and keeping the smaller details. Try not to over-smooth the foil or the whole process will need to be repeated.

4. Apply suitable adhesive before moulding the tin foil to the desired surface or object. In this example, Loctite has been applied to foamed PVC. To avoid any glue marks, start from the centre and smooth outwards when applying the tin foil, which will also help to keep the material nice and flat.

Once the tin foil has been prepared, apply it to the desired object using an appropriate adhesive. Take extra care not to tear the foil if moulding it around sharp corners.

The light reveals the mottling that is so key to a leathery texture.

The finished leather texture.

Drapes: Tin Foil and Kitchen Roll

This technique also uses tin foil but this time as a supporting base as opposed to the final texture. Two main issues arise when attempting to replicate drapery in miniature. The first is scale, as using most fabrics will instantly create a doll's house effect, where the pattern is too large for the object; the second is getting the material to conform accurately to the underlying surface.

This technique aims to address both issues by creating a realistic finish that precisely moulds and adapts to the underlying form while also making the texture completely customizable through painting and weathering.

MATERIALS AND EQUIPMENT

- Kitchen roll to form the drapes
- Tin foil to act as a protective underlayer and support
- Container for the water-down PVA mixture big enough to submerge the sheets of kitchen roll
- Old paintbrush to manipulate the kitchen roll as it dries; an old paintbrush is soft enough to avoid tearing the kitchen roll, which is especially fragile when wet
- Scalpel to clean up any rough edges and remove any exposed bits of tin foil

---

Pros

- A technique that is very difficult to get wrong, as the underlying tin foil means that any unsatisfactory finishes can be easily removed and replaced.
- Very realistic, as the weighted kitchen roll gathers beautifully on any surface.
- Uses common kitchen items
- Can be moulded to any surface very easily – the kitchen roll will not resist the way some stiffer fabrics would

Cons

- There is a risk of glue running all over the model from the soaked kitchen roll, so cover a much larger area than is needed with the tin foil and drain off some of the excess liquid before applying

- Moulding the tin foil to the underlying surface will run a further risk of damage to more delicate models.

Tips and Tricks

- Have a separate area where the soaked kitchen roll can drain off slightly to avoid any pooling on the model. This will also speed up drying times.
- One way of telling whether or not the kitchen roll has dried fully is simply to look at it – if it is slightly translucent and yellow, it has dried.
- Drop the kitchen roll slightly before lifting it back up and attaching it at the desired height to make the gather at the base more convincing.
- If the intention is to suspend fabric, consider tilting the whole model on its side so that the kitchen roll does not drop off.

Step-by-Step Method

1. Tear off a sheet of tin foil much larger than the intended area being covered and mould it as tightly as possible to the surface. Be careful to avoid any tears, as the PVA mixture will easily find its way through. Apply additional layers of tin foil if any such tears do appear.

Creating drapery with kitchen roll and tin foil.

2. Fill a container with a mixture of half PVA glue and half water. Mix thoroughly before submerging a sheet of kitchen roll into it. Strain the kitchen roll through your fingers to remove as much excess liquid as possible.

Cover the intended object in tin foil before starting. Then soak the kitchen roll in watered-down PVA and strain through your fingers to remove as much liquid as possible.

3. Drape the soaked kitchen roll onto the tin foil-covered surface. Pay close attention to image references to ensure that the material hangs authentically and, again, be as delicate as possible to avoid the kitchen roll tearing.

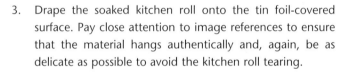

Drape the kitchen roll over the tin foil, embracing any folds that occur naturally. Cover a larger area than is desired and trim back as necessary.

4. Once the kitchen roll has dried, gently prise up the tin foil and lift the whole section clear. Trim the edges as desired, but leave the tin foil underneath the kitchen roll that is remaining to give it additional support and to assist with any further moulding that may be desired. The surface can now be painted and textured as appropriate.

Once dry, the tin foil and kitchen roll can be lifted off the object, trimmed to shape and painted. Take care not to damage the drapery as, even with the layers of kitchen roll and tin foil, it will still be quite delicate.

Depending on the weight of the fabric, the material may gather up with lots of folds or be quite stiff and relatively smooth.

Final drapery sample.

Soft Furnishings: Sponge and Kitchen Roll

Soft furnishings, such as cushions and pillows, often suffer from the same issues as drapery. The material they are made from often gives away the scale, they do not sit properly on surfaces and they are very difficult to texture in any way (applying paint to fabric can very quickly become a nightmare). This technique uses sponge as a base and kitchen roll to mould around the surface. It can get a little messy, but the result means that objects such as cushions can realistically sink back into a surface.

MATERIALS AND EQUIPMENT

- Sponge cloths
- Pen to mark the sponge for cutting; a pencil will not suffice here and a Sharpie is not ideal, as it will bleed heavily into the kitchen roll
- PVA glue
- Kitchen roll to cover the underlying sponge and seal the surface
- Old paintbrush to press the kitchen roll into the sponge and help shape it
- Scalpel with a sharp blade
- Scissors to trim the edges of the pillow or cushion while the kitchen roll is still slightly damp

---

Pros

- A very realistic technique that will make soft furnishings sit convincingly on a surface.
- Easy to get a production line going and churn out a good number of these
- Uses common kitchen items
- Completely scalable, not just in size but also in the texture of the tissue that is being used

Cons

- Too much glue will risk the kitchen roll tearing, which cannot subsequently be easily disguised.

- Too much glue will also mean that it will seep through the kitchen roll while the object is drying and glue the it to the underlying surface. This will ruin the surface

Tips and Tricks

- Apply less glue than you think necessary to avoid excess seeping through the kitchen roll. More can easily be added later.
- Keep hands as clean as possible – any glue on them will make shaping the kitchen roll almost impossible.
- For smaller scales, consider using a toilet roll with less texture for a more realistic finish. Kitchen roll at smaller scales can lead to a more knitted texture.
- Cover the area where the object will sit with tin foil – similar to the drapery technique above – to help it to mould more realistically to its form.

Step-by-Step Method

1. Take a sponge cloth and mark out a piece of the desired size. Depending on the thickness of the pillow or cushion that you are creating, several pieces may need to be cut out and layered together.

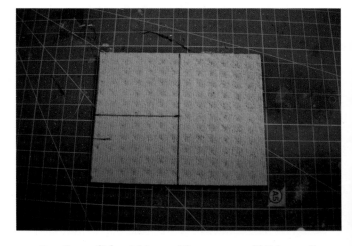

Creating soft furnishings with sponge and kitchen roll.

2. Using a scalpel, preferably with a new blade, trim around the edges of the sponge to create a softer, more realistic edge. If seat cushions are being made, just trimming the very edges may be all that is required. Do not worry about how messy the edge subsequently looks – this will all be hidden and add to the natural finish.

Two pieces of sponge cloth are glued together and, once dry, shaped and trimmed as necessary. Ignore any rough edges – these will actually add to the final effect.

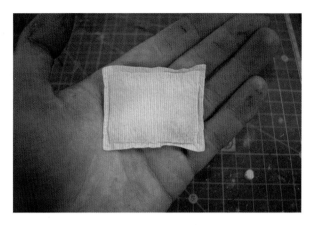

Once dry, the edges can be trimmed to the desired length and, in some cases, the object can be folded and moulded a little more into shape.

3. Apply some PVA glue to the sponge on one side and cover with a sheet of kitchen roll. Use an old paintbrush to press it into the surface, not your finger, as any glue that has found its way on to your hand will quickly ruin the effect. Repeat on the other side.

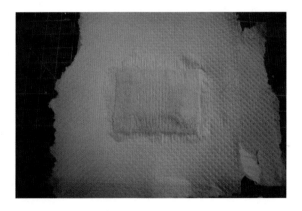

Cover one side of the sponge with PVA before adhering a piece of kitchen roll. Repeat on the other side and then pinch the edges together. Avoid using too much PVA otherwise it will soak through and risk tearing the kitchen roll.

4. Using a finger, pinch the ends of the kitchen roll together and trim using a pair of scissors. An extra amount of PVA can be applied using a cocktail stick if the edges come apart whilst cutting. Fold the edges gently by pressing your finger against them to create a more defined crease, and then leave to dry.

The cushions on this sofa do not stand perfectly on end, but mould and sink into the surface.

Final soft furnishing sample.

Carpets: Sponge, Sandpaper, Mixed Herbs and Fabric

Carpets are a bit of a headscratcher for many. Most students will opt to simply print off a desired pattern or texture and glue the paper down onto the floor. While this is a very quick and easy solution, the final finish is often far from satisfactory.

There are a number of solutions lying about the home that will not only offer much needed texture but are also just as easy to apply as gluing a sheet of paper. The four methods described here are good examples. You only need to consider the scale and the thickness of the chosen material to avoid any offset measurements or, as always, the dreaded doll's house effect.

MATERIALS AND EQUIPMENT

- Sponge cloths
- Sandpaper
- Mixed dried herbs to make wool rugs
- Fabrics – in this instance, a piece of old clothing was used for method 4
- Adhesive – the ideal adhesive will differ for each material used
- Scalpel to cut the sandpaper and sponge
- Scissors to trim and shape the fabric

Pros

- These techniques will add some much-needed texture to an often-overlooked part of a model
- These individual techniques will allow the maker to tackle a wide range of scales
- Easy to paint, weather and customise as desired
- Just as easy to apply as gluing a sheet of paper

Cons

- Some of these techniques will not be viable if a continuous sheet is needed for larger-scale builds
- If a printed pattern is desired, either painting by hand or transfers are the best option, but of course require additional steps

Tips and Tricks

- When using the sponge, keep the edges as neat as possible. Using a new scalpel blade will help greatly with this.
- When using the sandpaper, avoid creasing it, as this will show in the painting and be almost impossible to remove.
- When using mixed herbs, avoid using too much PVA to prevent it from pooling all over the model.
- When using the fabric, iron out any creases prior to adhesion.

Four Methods for Creating Carpet

1. For the first method, cut out a piece of sponge cloth, ensuring that the edges are as neat as possible. Cover one side with adhesive and apply to the intended area. This technique works best on larger builds and for thicker carpets.

Creating carpets using sponge, sandpaper, mixed herbs and fabric.

2. For method two, cut a sheet of sandpaper to the intended floorplan. Cut as delicately as possible, as any creases will show noticeably when painted. Apply to the intended area, ideally with double-sided tape to stop the paper warping. This technique is ideal for medium- to small-scale builds and for more dense carpets.

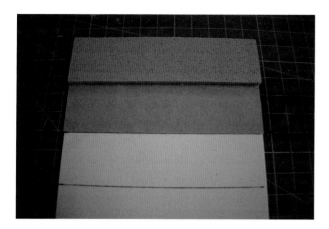

Sponge can be glued directly to a surface on larger-scale models to simulate carpets, while for small-scale models a sheet of sandpaper will usually suffice. Ideally, these should be laid first, before any wall details, as skirting boards or wall panelling can then hide any messy edges.

3. If wool rugs are needed, mix some herbs with PVA into a thick paste and smear over a sheet of tin foil. Shape the mixture as desired and leave to dry. Once dried, peel off the herb strip and glue to the desired area. The herbs, when painted, will blend together visually to create the impression of a thick, textured surface.

Mixed herbs are a great way of mimicking wool rugs or similar textures, and simply require mixing up with PVA glue. Fabrics are a great option for any textured or pattern carpets, and only need to be cut to size.

4. For the final method, take an old piece of clothing and cut out a section larger than is needed. Glue to the surface and then trim using a scalpel. The fabric in the example here was chosen to replicate a typical office or school flooring. Paint as necessary.

With all of these techniques, priming is essential before going in with a base colour, as there are many areas where gaps can show through.

Carpets contain a wealth of texture that is often poorly represented in miniature models.

Final carpet sample.

Panelling: Card

Panelling can be found in a number of places, both outside and inside, including doors, shop fronts, interior walls and more. Panelling is one of the simpler jobs a model maker will undertake, with the only real frustration arising from the time it takes to build up all of the individual layers. Yet modellers often use expensive materials that are just not necessary.

The technique described here uses card as a substitute for materials such as styrene, as card is much cheaper (free if found from the recycling) and contains a small amount of texture that makes it especially effective for wood panelling. Care needs to be taken with the edges, which can be easily damaged, but otherwise this technique is pretty failsafe.

MATERIALS AND EQUIPMENT

- Card, recycled if possible
- Pencil
- Glue (a glue stick is best)
- Scalpel to cut out the panels; avoid using scissors, as these will bend the card

---

Pros

- Free if finding card from out of the recycling
- Very quick and easy with no real drying times
- The texture of the card will add a little bit of interest to almost every scale
- A good opportunity to practise precise measuring and cutting

Cons

- The edges of the card can be easily damaged; sealing them with a small amount of glue will help to prevent this
- The card can warp if not securely attached to the main surface or if a water-based glue such as PVA is used

Tips and Tricks

- Check, double-check and triple-check measurements, as a single millimetre can offset an entire wall of panelling.
- Build up the layers of panelling on the main surface itself. Creating the panelling separately and then attaching it to the main wall will encourage warping.
- If possible, extend the panelling out slightly from the main build and then trim once complete. This will avoid any frustrating gaps at the ends of walls or in corners.
- Use a brand-new scalpel blade and rotate frequently – blunt blades can create burrs even in card.

Step-by-Step Method

1. Start by creating a template of the panelling section that you are intending to create. This will act as a useful reference when building up the individual layers. Next, draw out the panels needed. Biro has been used here for clarity but use pencil where possible, as biro can bleed through certain paints.

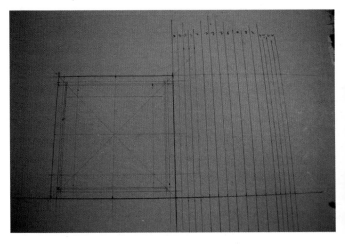

Creating wall panelling using card.

2. Cut out the panels and store them in groups on a flat surface. Try not to mix up different sizes, as this will lead to mistakes that may or may not be rectifiable.

A wall panel design is drawn up on a sheet of cereal box card before the individual pieces are cut out using a scalpel blade. Special care should be taken to avoid damaging any edges, as this will become extremely noticeable when the panels are assembled.

3. Thinking about construction is essential for panelling. Complete each layer before moving on to the next. If using PVA, have a damp cotton bud to hand to clean up any excess glue that is squeezed out when adhering pieces to one another.

Measuring is crucial with panelling, so take the time to correctly measure any angles and use whatever tools and templates are required.

4. Once the panelling is complete, leave it to dry. Weigh it down, if possible, under a heavy object or book to prevent warping. There is no need to seal the surface: simply prime and paint.

Layer up the panelling from smallest to largest, always ensuring each piece has a solid, even base and that the entire surface is coated in glue, otherwise you will run the risk of edges curling up after painting.

Panelling is so diverse and, depending on the formations, different combinations of materials may be needed to most accurately represent it.

Final panelling sample.

PART III: PROJECTS

CHAPTER 8

CREATING A MINIATURE GRAMOPHONE USING FOUND OBJECTS

The focus of the previous chapters has been on using found materials to create texture samples for both practice and as reference. Now it is time to focus on some actual projects where these skills may be applied in full.

This first will focus entirely on the process of kit bashing – the use of model kits parts and found objects to build up shape and form. A true understanding of this process can only be achieved through practice. Its experimental, surprising and often chaotic nature not only renders almost all planning futile, but will make every single build completely unique and, hopefully, a wonderful experience.

This project will attempt to create a gramophone using only found objects and materials. The intention is to show the effectiveness of the kit-bashing technique and that authentic results are indeed possible, although there is always some degree of 'accidental' detail.

The Build

1. The starting point, as with most builds, was determining what scale the model should be produced at. The approach I chose to take with this was to identify the gramophone component that would have most influence on this, see what I had available in my parts collection

and then work backwards, determining the scale from the chosen object. Subsequently, I identified the horn as this key component, which I then matched to a plastic candlestick holder, which would scale up to ⅑ scale.

Kit bashing a miniature gramophone.

2. Kit bashing is so heavily dependent upon the analysis of the available objects that the majority of time spent on such builds is taken up by simply deciding which items to use. Take the candlestick holder. It had a great shape, a smooth surface and the plastic was reasonably thick, meaning it should hold up well to any rough handling. However, there was a clear mould line down either side, and the top end

of the holder did not taper enough to accurately create the horn shape that was needed. While 'accidental' detail is a key feature of kit bashing, it should not be used as an excuse. Both of these issues needed addressing.

The gramophone horn starts to take shape using plastic found objects. It is important to rinse every component in warm, soapy water prior to use to remove any dirt and grime.

3. To that end, I proceeded by cutting away roughly half of the candlestick holder and sanding down the mould lines. To create the horn shape I was looking for, I cut off the end of a balloon pump, dug out a small plastic chess piece lying at the bottom of one of my 'bits' boxes and secured them in place with superglue. Superglue was essential here – plastic weld, after testing, did not work well with bonding these components, though it did serve a purpose in smoothing out some of the scratch marks left over from some over-zealous sanding on the pump piece.

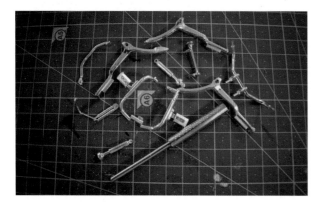

Spare model kit parts are a great way of building up detail very quickly without adding too much weight to the overall build.

4. The first tricky moment came when looking for a way to curve the horn around to form the elbow that would then be attached to the tone arm and bracket. The end of the horn had already been cut to roughly a 60-degree angle to accommodate this. My hope lay in a collection of parts left over from a commission that had involved a motorcycle kit. While I was able to find a curved component to make up one section of the elbow, it did not have sufficient surface area to bond effectively to the horn; it simply would not have withstood the weight.

Details do not always need to be built up using a single object, but can be created using a mixture of smaller pieces. While this requires more work, it often leads to better form and detail.

5. This issue was fixed by rummaging around in a box of old camera parts and unearthing a small plastic gear and tube. These made the elbow much thicker and also assisted in narrowing the horn shape more naturally.

In this example, three components from different sources are combined to form the elbow of the gramophone horn.

6. When assembled, it turned out I had accidently created part of the swivel mechanism for the tone arm at the same time. While I was using various image references throughout the course of this build, these satisfying, unplanned moments are what make this process so enjoyable. One end of the elbow component was sanded to provide extra grip when it was then secured to the horn section, again using superglue.

Some early issues started to arise in the form of messy edges. These would be solved later through the application of rubber strips taken from a motorcycle model kit.

7. It is important to be critical and fair with one's work throughout the build process. In this instance, I was very happy with the overall shape that had been formed and the level of detail, but there were two elements I was not satisfied with. The first was the overhanging part of the red horn component. The second was the rough edges between each individual component that made up the horn itself. I was unsure exactly how best to proceed at this stage, so I left it until more of the build had been completed.

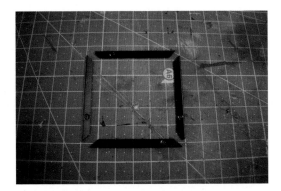

An initial frame was made from parts of polaroid film cartridge. This is a good example of embracing accidental detail – the moulded pin marks would later be disguised as knots in the wood.

8. The next stage was to move onto the turntable and box. Alongside model making, I am also a Polaroid enthusiast, meaning I have plenty of empty film cartridges lying around. The film doors, I discovered when fiddling one day, are quite easy to remove, and in this instance formed a great trim for the base of the box. An odd place to start, perhaps, but what caught my attention most of all was the moulding mark on each one of them – if painted correctly, these could give the impression of knots in the wood.

Sometimes the choice of which component to use is based more upon practicality than aesthetics. An earplug container is used to build up the main section of the gramophone box. The shape is not ideal but the thick plastic will create a strong platform.

9. An object was desperately needed to form the main body of the gramophone box. To that end, I sourced a small plastic container that had once housed some earplugs. The corners were slightly more rounded than I would have liked but the sides sloped at a nice angle, the plastic was slightly frosted, giving a nicely textured surface to paint on, and – above all – it was sturdy enough to support the weight of the rest of the build. A couple of layers of cereal box card were added on top of the Polaroid frame, which was then secured to the base of the earplug container.

Layers of card, plastic and other material are moulded to add the decorative panelling on the box.

10. To form the top panel of the box, I considered using cereal box card again, but was concerned that, with handling, the edges would quickly become damaged. To address this issue, I found a used gift card, which I cut into shape. Several layers were made before a big, chunky plastic base that would have once supported a model was found to finish it off. This layering created a firm platform onto which the gramophone horn would be secured – another good reason for not using card.

The gramophone base starting to take shape, already using different material sources.

11. Despite my reluctance to use card earlier, my continued use of plastic was presenting a problem – there was no surface texture. I wanted some form of grain-like texture so the gramophone did not look new. Old, damaged, weathered objects are beautiful to look at, not only because of the visual interest but also because of the story all that damage tells. Therefore I cut a slightly small section of card

and adhered it to the top of the box. The smaller section meant that the edges would not get damaged while the texture of the card would give some impression of wood grain when lightly painted.

I was luckily able to source a turntable from a single moulded plastic wheel.

12. The search for a turntable was the hardest of all. I was determined to find this piece in one single object, and not layer together various other pieces as I had done with every other section of the build. I tried printer parts, bottle tops, even coins, but they were all either too large, too small or too thick. The problem was solved with a component whose origins I have long since forgotten, but I would imagine that it came from either an old camera or something like a DVD player. It had a lot of unnecessary detail, but the moulded numbers and rings gave a record vibe and I decided not to remove them as I had done with the moulded lines in the candlestick base.

Feet are fashioned from an electrical connector block. No blending is required, as the majority of this will be hidden.

13. The base of the gramophone did not sit flush in many of the image references that I was studying, so I looked for ways to add some feet. I was tempted to use some model kit parts; however there was a distinct lack of circuitry in the build so far which was quickly corrected with some little arms taken from a connector block. They were chosen for their detail and angled form, which I was sure would give the impression of some elegant moulding when painted gold. These were simply superglued in place.

A motorcycle kit piece makes a good substitute for a bracket, both in aesthetic and in strength. The horn, by this point, was relatively heavy and required a sturdy support.

14. With a significant proportion of the box now completed, I turned my attention back to the gramophone horn and the next issue – how to secure it to the base. I found a motorcycle kit component – a foot peg – which was just about the correct size and shape but most importantly had a decent surface area either end to support the weight of the horn. It again had some nice moulded detail, which, when painted, would give a more traditional feel, especially when covered with a wash.

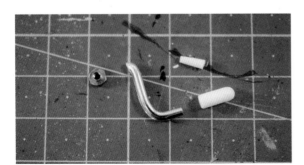

A crank was created from a nut, a model kit piece and a plastic game component. Connecting the plastic to the metal nut was made possible with Loctite.

15. Completion of the gramophone box was now only held back by the crank. In a similar way to the elbow, I sought to combine several components together to build up the correct form. Again, I found a good amount of the shape in a motorcycle kit component, but both ends needed embellishing with some detail. A battleship game pin gave the clean curved handle section, while a random brass nut formed the ideal connecting piece to the box itself.

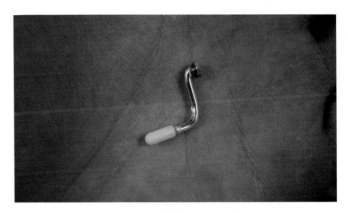

The final assembly of the gramophone crank. Again, this was a build that could have possibly been satisfied with a single component, but much more detail and accuracy was achieved this way.

16. When all the parts of the handle were glued together, I noticed that the join between the crank and the nut was a little rough. To fix this, I used a needle file to very gently round the edge off. A small amount of plastic weld was then applied. This was not to assist with adhesion, but to smooth off any faint scratch marks that had been left in the surface of the handle by the needle file. Once finished, the handle was then glued to the side of the box.

The starter pieces for the sound box, which would connect to the end of the tone arm.

17. At the same time, I had been rummaging around in a box of camera parts and a very small plastic tub of old watch components, where I found two pieces that seemed to come together to form the perfect sound box (the round section at the end of the tone arm with the needle). I was amused by the camera button, which had 'on/off' moulded into the surface – particularly apt for the build at hand. However, the other side needed to have some moulded slots, which a watch cog seemed to provide rather well. I was hesitant to use superglue in this instance, as I was concerned that it would frost over the cog and hide some of the detail. Therefore I decided to attach the cog to the plastic button using plastic weld, which gave just enough adhesion to keep it in place. Painting would finish the job.

Plastic weld is not the adhesive to use when trying to bond metal and plastic; however, the brass cog in this instance was so light that the plastic weld was sufficient to simply hold it in place.

18. The curved piece attached to the on/off button had been cut off. This led to another accident – it formed the perfect extension to the tone arm. A small stanchion from a model ship kit formed a good substitute for a needle, and was attached to the sound box using plastic weld. The final construction was then superglued to the main horn and lifted slightly at an angle to accommodate the record, which I would build at a later date.

The finished assembly. The horn was left detached from the base to assist in the painting and finishing stages and to reduce the risk of damage.

19. The construction phase was now complete, and I was fairly satisfied with how the build had turned out. The turntable and bike handle had provided the most 'accidental' detail, but I was confident that, with a lick of paint, these features would give the build some character without damaging its credibility. The horn and the box were deliberately left separate for two reasons: to make the painting stage easier, and to ensure that the horn did not snap off from the strain during painting.

Both assemblies were primed using a paintbrush. An airbrush would have resulted in a better finish, but I do not think that this is essential.

20. In most similar instances, I would have used an airbrush not only to prime but also complete the majority of the paintwork. However, good results can be achieved perfectly

well with a traditional paintbrush and, as this book is all about accessibility, a paint brush seemed appropriate. For the primer, I used Vallejo Surface Primer in black, which I applied in two thin layers. It is important when applying primer not to apply too much in one go, as the paint can very easily pool and ruin the surface of a model. It's better to be patient and create a nice, even finish.

The first layer of gold was painted on. A thin metallic paint, it needed several layers to be applied to achieve significant depth of colour. A white base coat would have assisted with this, but with this build, white areas could have easily been left exposed after the painting process.

21. Once the primer had dried and cured fully, I started painting the gramophone horn and feet. The first layer consisted of Vallejo Model Air in gold, again applied with a paintbrush. A common issue with metallic paints is that they are fairly translucent – mixing them with a white or any other more opaque colour often corrects this. However, as mentioned previously, I did not want a clean, perfect finish, so I applied about three layers of the gold until only a few faint patches of the black remained. When covered in a wash, these would blend in and create some satisfying gradation.

Additional tones and definition were built up through the application of several heavy washes.

22. The first wash was a Citadel Shade in Reikland Fleshshade. I applied significantly more than I would usually, as I wanted the pooling to help define some of the moulding and add depth. While the first coat created a satisfactory effect, I wanted this to be even stronger, so I applied another wash but this time with a Vallejo Wash in dark brown. This also added some more colour variation to take away that new finish.

The same painting process was used for the base – all acrylics and washes.

23. The painting process was much the same for the rest of the build. Any silver areas were washed heavily in greys and blacks, all from either the Vallejo or Citadel range. All the washes were much heavier than I would normally apply to add greater colour variation. For the turntable in particular, a lot of my image references depicted very worn surfaces, which I attempted to replicate with heavy washes of black followed by a faint dry brushing of a slightly lighter tone of the original colour. The whole gramophone horn was drybrushed with a gold mixed with a small amount of white to take away some of the shine left over from the washes.

Once the paintwork was finished, the two assemblies were glued together and the project was complete.

24. Once the paint had been allowed to dry and cure fully, it was time to attach the gramophone horn to the box. A small amount of superglue was applied in order to avoid spoiling the surrounding paintwork. The only thing that was left to be added was a small record that was made from a small scrap of card, and the build was complete.

Summary

Overall, I was very pleased with this build. All of the components that had been used had not been chosen because they were the only ones available but because they actually supported a specific element of the project. This is always one of the most satisfying parts of the kit-bashing process: when the right piece comes along. So much time can be spent in frustration at not being able to find anything that matches what is needed, but often the search does bear fruit.

There were of course moments of dissatisfaction, and it is important in our learning and understanding of model making to reflect on these regardless of the situation. Greater accuracy could have been achieved by placing a smaller component under the turntable to lift it clear of the base, which may have also created a nicer finish around the edge. The build-up of wash does go some way to assist with this, but it could have been nicer without. The mould marks on the inside of the gramophone horn add a nice extra detail that reminds the audience that this object has been fabricated from found components – a feature which is very important to me when using this technique.

The finished assembly. The horn was left detached from the base to assist in the painting and finishing stages and to reduce the risk of damage.

TIPS

If it is your intention to attempt to replicate a similar object using this technique, I would advise the following:

- Gather together as many objects as possible before starting the build, as constantly getting up to source objects you do not have can become very tedious and frustrating.
- Determine exactly what finish you intend to create prior to the build, as this will influence the standard to which pieces are cut, sanded and glued very early on.
- Persevere – whether or not you have chosen the correct piece, or combined things in a satisfactory way, will only be revealed after that first layer of primer has been allowed to dry. Have faith in the process and your ability, and see it through!
- Some objects, depending on where they have been sourced from and how they have been handled, may require cleaning in warm soapy water prior to use to remove any dirt and grime.
- Dry-fitting is essential with this method of making, so only apply glue once you are absolutely certain of which objects you intend to use.

CREATING A SCALE SET USING RECYCLED CARD

The gramophone build has shown what can be possible when building something using a wide range of different objects and components. However, building up a resource bank of all these different items takes time, so those who are just starting out in the hobby may find this limits what they can create.

This second project, therefore, will focus purely on a found material that everyone will have at least a small collection of – card. One of the most simple and familiar materials out there, it often forms the bulk of a typical household's recycling. Used as food packaging, labels, postal packaging and more, it is a very accessible material. Many modellers do not believe that professional and sturdy results can be achieved with card, which is unfortunate as we have already seen in Chapter 2 just how many different applications it can have.

In this project, I will be building a small corner set in which to display the gramophone build from the previous chapter. This will be kept as simple as possible to ensure that everyone can follow the steps as an effective starter project. All the card will be sourced from recycling and the project will use several of the techniques we have explored previously.

The Build

1. The corner set will be built at ⅑ scale to match the gramophone kit-bashing build. For the walls, I chose to use theatre flats as a guideline. A standard flat is simply a sheet of timber attached to a rectangular wooden frame, and

typically measures 4ft feet wide by 8ft tall (122 × 244cm). In ⅑ scale this equates to 135.5 × 271mm, and these were the dimensions of the two walls I would be building.

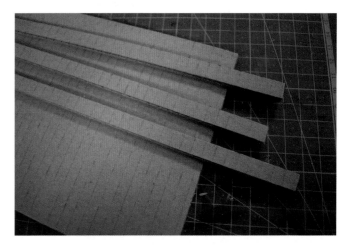

Creating a scale set using found materials.

2. Starting off the build, I chose to use a two-step process to construct the walls. The first step would be to build a base structure using thick brown packaging card, while the second step would involve cladding that structure in a thinner cereal box-type card to add extra strength and to create a smooth surface on which to add detail and to paint. I cut out a sheet of cardboard measuring 135.5 × 271mm, followed by four strips that would form the wall edges, each measuring 10mm deep.

Brown packaging card was used to make the base of the set walls. To add strength and to prevent warping, braces were attached on the sides and across the centre using hot glue.

3. As I wanted to avoid as much warping as possible, I used a glue gun to stick the cardboard strips to the reverse of the wall face. Extra supports were added – one going straight across the centre with two additional angled braces above and below. These add extra strength to a single flat piece of cardboard, leading to a more professional finish.

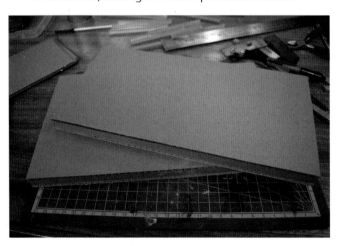

The two completed walls. They were still prone to damage and warping at this stage, so additional steps were required.

4. Once the wall side strips and centre supports were glued in place, the reverse face was applied, essentially forming a solid cardboard box. This whole process was then repeated to create two solid walls. Note the corrugated edges on the sides of the walls. They can be quite unsightly once it gets to the painting stage, which is another good reason for going on to clad the walls.

The two walls were attached together with more hot glue. Any offsets could be hidden later behind wall panelling and extra details.

5. The two walls were then joined together. At the base of the left-hand wall there was a slight offset of about a millimetre, which had been created as a result of the bottom edge being slightly angled. This was not a major concern, as it could be easily covered up with another layer of card. Larger offsets would have created structural issues, but those would have been more noticeable before this point.

A base was constructed using the same method as for the wall. It's important to account for the thickness of the walls if they sit on top of the base, otherwise the dimensions will be off.

6. The exact same construction method was used for the diorama base. If objects of substantial weight were being added later, it would be advisable to add extra supports through the centre of the base to prevent any sagging. In this instance, only the gramophone was being added, so there was no need for this.

upper section accompanied with card wall panelling below, meaning the wall would effectively be cladded anyway. Consider cladding the whole face if you intend to approach this build differently. Lines were drawn out marking where the bricks would be placed, leaving a sufficient gap for the mortar.

A thinner cereal box card was used to clad the edges of the set. This added strength and another protective layer to prevent damage to the edges.

7. The next step focused on applying the thinner card as a protective cladding. Strips of cereal box card were cut out to match the depth of the original walls and glued in place using a glue gun. These strips needed to be flush otherwise they would either stick out, meaning they would be prone to damage, or there would be a gap, which would be extremely noticeable once painted. Try to avoid trimming off any excess after application (which has been advised several times through the examples in Part II), as on a build like this it would be very difficult to get a straight, clean edge.

Guidelines were marked on the upper section of the walls for the first layer of texture – brickwork.

8. With the edges protected, I would normally continue to clad the entire front and reverse faces of the walls. However, the plan was to have card brickwork on the

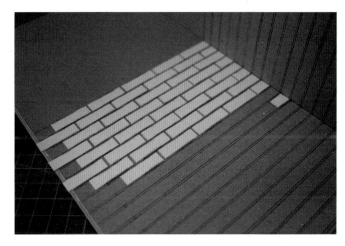

Bricks were cut out of the same card used for the cladding and arranged in rows using superglue. Gaps were left for mortar.

9. Individual bricks were cut out of more cereal box card before being glued into place. Bricks towards the edge were allowed to overhang slightly, as, with such a short piece of material, these can indeed be trimmed off after application. The bricks were glued to the surface individually using superglue, which is also effective in sealing the edges and preventing them from fraying.

The completed brickwork. Notice how the bricks extend over the edges of the walls. This was to ensure a nice even fit when they were later trimmed down with a scalpel.

10. Once the brickwork was completed, it was time to plan out the rest of the build. A gap was deliberately left at the top of the wall to account for the ceiling moulding, while the lower section would be completely taken up with half-height wall panelling. Notice how some of the bricks have ink stains from being marked out with a biro. Avoid this where possible, as it can go on to ruin later paintwork, or ensure that you are using a black primer to obscure it.

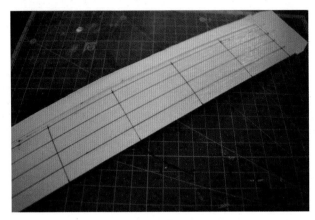

For the floor, planks were drawn out to scale on cereal box card and then textured using a glue stick. They were then left to dry. Any warping could be ignored, as the planks would straighten out when applied to the base.

11. As I wanted the wall panelling to sit on top of the flooring, the floorboards needed to come next. I used the glue stick technique (*see* Chapter 6) to texture the individual boards. As the previous example of this had been weathered slightly through some heavy dry-brushing, I chose this time to go for a more as-new finish.

Ready-mixed filler was applied to the brickwork and smeared into the gaps. It's best to use a flexible tool for this to avoid damaging the surface of the brickwork.

12. While the floorboards were drying after having the glue stick applied to them, I went in with the ready-mixed filler acting as the mortar for the brickwork. Where the ceiling moulding met the brickwork at the top of the wall there was a lot of debris; however, this was not an issue as the ceiling moulding would sit on top of the brickwork. For the wall panelling below, I did not want this debris so I placed down two panels of card to create a nice, even join between the two textures. Following this, a damp sponge was used to wipe the surface and remove the excess filler while giving more definition to the brickwork.

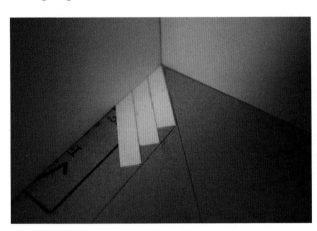

Once the floorboards had dried, they were trimmed and glued to the baseboard in a herringbone pattern. Guidelines were once again marked out to assist with the texture placement.

13. Leaving the filler to dry, I moved back to the floorboards. These were cut at an angle to create a herringbone effect and were simply glued one by one using superglue. Superglue was used to ensure that there was absolutely no chance the edges of the boards could lift up; several washes would be applied to the flooring, which would otherwise pose an increased risk of this happening.

The completed pattern. Biro was used here to mark out the floorboards for clarity, but this is not recommended in practice as it can easily show through paintwork. Use a pencil wherever possible.

14. Once the floorboards were all laid, the next step was to start putting in the first layer of wall panelling. By applying this after the floor, the panelling could hide any uneven edges at the base of the wall. In this instance, there was not much to hide but previous experience has shown that leaving this option open is invaluable. Note the numbers written on the individual wall panels – these are to mark the width of each piece to ensure that there can be no confusion.

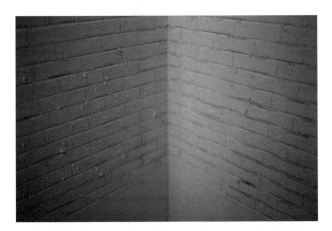

The surface of the bricks were wiped with a damp sponge to remove as much surface filler as possible. This disturbed the surface of the brickwork and created some debris, which was easily removed with a brush.

15. After the filler was allowed to dry fully, it was noticeable that some debris had formed on the brickwork as a result of the friction of the sponge moving over the card surface. This was no problem at all and could actually be quite

beneficial texturally. The debris was removed with a tooth-brush, and the roughened surface would add some extra interest during the painting process.

Wall panelling was built up using more card. This is a key example of how the thickness of the card being used needs to be monitored to ensure accuracy of scale. If it's too thin or too thick, this will become very noticeable very quickly.

16. There were four layers of wall panelling in total, which were glued one by one using a glue stick. Superglue was not the best option here, as a significant amount of it would be needed and, more importantly, I needed time to adjust the panels as they were applied to the surface. One wrong move with superglue would have caused a world of trouble.

The completed set build, finished off with ceiling trim and skirting board.

17. The final build, complete with ceiling moulding: it was quite simple but a good demonstration of how versatile card is and the quality that can be achieved. Some of the sides were a little rough and uneven but the intention was to create a protective box/framework in which the gramophone could be displayed, so this was of no great concern.

As the intention of the set was not only to demonstrate the use of card but also to display the gramophone build, a simple table was mocked up using several found objects.

18. To accompany the build and to give the gramophone something to sit on in the corner diorama, I kit bashed a simple round table using, from top to bottom: a Pringles tube lid, a salt dispenser lid, a plastic connector, an empty plastic ball bearing case and the second candlestick base which made the pair from the gramophone build. These pieces were chosen based upon how well they connected with one another, as I wanted to ensure that the table formed a solid support for the gramophone (which was relatively heavy in comparison).

The whole set primed and ready for painting.

19. Once everything had been left to dry for a day or so, both the corner diorama and table were primed using a Vallejo Surface Primer in black and painted using the same techniques shown in the previous build project.

Summary

The purpose of this build was to showcase how simple card can be used to notable effect. Many a time, a student has come back to me with carrier bags filled with all sorts of materials that they have just purchased, only to be left utterly perplexed when asked the simple question – what are you going to use them for? Even if they have something in mind, it rarely concerns a situation that cannot be adequately solved with something as rudimentary and cheap as card. At the other end of the scale, the more experienced often turn away from card because it is a 'basic' material, which cannot possibly achieve quality results.

This project could have been taken much further – shelves, cupboards, desks, window frames, doorways and more could have been included. However, what has been constructed will hopefully go some way to demonstrate that it is an understanding of the material, not the material itself, that forms the foundation of a good model.

Final set build.

TIPS

If it is your intention to attempt to replicate a similar build using card, I would advise the following:

- Collect as many thicknesses of card as possible to give more flexibility when creating objects, panelling or a strong foundation.
- Check for creases or damage before working with card, as it is easy to become distracted when focusing on other elements.
- Be mindful of the drawing implement you are using – biro has pros and cons.
- Look after the edges – the first thing that will ruin a card build is damaged edges. Protect them by either ensuring that the surrounding environment is clear of any objects that could be knocked or by sealing the edges once each piece of card has been applied to the build.
- Build a solid base – not just for structural reasons but also to avoid card's nemesis: warping.

CHAPTER 10

CREATING A SCENIC DIORAMA USING HOUSEHOLD MATERIALS

There are few greater examples of the wealth of possible model-making techniques than model railways. From industrial docklands to country moorland, the world of railway modelling has covered everything there is to model. Consequently, the range of modelling materials focused specifically on this hobby is colossal, ranging from scatter and static grass to styrene brickwork and laser-cut kits.

However, one complication that every railway modeller will have encountered is the sheer amount of these materials that is needed. To model a scene accurately, every element needs to be accounted for, and, regardless of the size of the layout being built, investing in the required materials can become an expensive endeavour.

This final project looks not only to reduce the cost to railway modellers but also to show that, although it may be tempting to purchase pre-made materials and avoid the effort, many of those materials can be easily made at home. Many of the techniques from Part II can be combined in various ways to create beautiful scenic elements that are just as good as, if not better than, retail alternatives. Of course, although the focus here is on railway modelling, these techniques apply equally well to other areas, such as wargaming or creating dioramas for model kits.

The Build

1. Determining the scale of this small scenic diorama was a much simpler process as you can follow the existing model railway gauges. The ones with which I was most familiar were OO and N gauge, having modelled in both scales

myself. The techniques I intended to use could work easily with any scale, I decided to model in OO, as it is one of the most popular and readily available.

Creating a scenic diorama using household materials.

2. To start, I gathered some image references that would assist in the modelling of a small riverbank scene. To create the elevated section of track, I found some polystyrene packaging, which was cut up and glued down to a base using hot glue. Although polystyrene can create the most awful mess, it is very easy to shape with the most basic of tools, and using it in scenes such as this is a great way of recycling it.

A base for the river bank was made using a piece of polystyrene covered in a layer of ready-mixed filler.

3.   The scene was then coated in a layer of ready-mixed filler to create a stronger surface upon which to place the remaining elements and also to smooth out and fill the rough edges of the polystyrene. Varying the amount of filler applied in different areas was a great way of adding natural interest; in the thin areas, small balls of polystyrene came through and became more defined rocks, while the thicker areas formed the natural mud slopes and river bank. This was allowed to dry completely before moving on to the next stage.

OO gauge is one of the most common in railway modelling. A short section of track was laid down using wood glue.

4.   A small section of OO track was glued down using wood glue. Superglue is not advisable, as it will not leave much time to adjust the track if positioned incorrectly. Wood glue also has the added bonus of being thick enough to act as a filler should the track be raised ever so slightly off

the base. This was allowed to dry completely before adding the ballast. While the ballast could have been applied while the track was still being secured, allowing the wood glue to dry reduced the risk of the track moving during application and creating a mess.

Ballast was made using the filler technique. A small amount of paint was mixed into the ballast before spreading it over the track to add a little colour variation.

5.   The ballast was made by spreading ready-mixed filler out onto baking paper, allowing it to dry, cracking it up, placing it through a sieve and then mixing with a small amount of acrylic paint to add some colour variation. It was then spread out along the track. No glue was applied, as this will be dropped on to the ballast once it has been 'arranged'. Some of the particles had clumped together as a result of the added paint. While these could have been kept to act as larger rocks by the trackside, they were ultimately removed due to personal preference.

Diluted PVA was dropped onto the ballast; as it soaked in, it secured the ballast in place.

6. A drop of washing-up liquid was added to a fifty-fifty mixture of PVA glue and water, and this solution was then dropped onto the ballast using a pipette. The reason the solution was applied after covering the track with the ballast was that the adhesive could seep through the ballast and glue everything in place. If glue was applied first, only the very bottom particles of ballast would be secured. The drop of washing-up liquid serves to break the surface tension of the water. Not adding this would have resulted in the mixture briefly rolling on the surface of the ballast and disturbing the particles. A suitable alternative to adding washing-up liquid is to spray a fine mist of water over the scene to saturate the ballast prior to applying the adhesive.

The whole diorama, minus the track, was primed before a base coat was applied to the ballast. The ballast could have been stained with washes, but this technique allows for greater customisation.

The danger of applying too much adhesive was that it would run out from under the edges and dislodge the ballast.

7. In some areas, due to the uneven surface and adding slightly too much adhesive, the solution had pooled on the surface and then run down the river bank. While glue marks were no concern at this point, the disturbed ballast that had moved away was. Although this would have been easy to correct with an old paintbrush, this was actually left to dry. As with so many natural scenes, neatness is the enemy!

8. After the ballast had dried (which could take several days depending on the temperature of the room and the amount of adhesive that had been applied), the entire scene bar the rails was primed with a Vallejo Surface Primer in black. While this is not necessary for railway modelling per say, wargamers especially will likely do this to seal the surface of a character base. Once the primer had dried, I applied a base colour to the ballast and sleepers.

Once the base coat was dry, washes were used to bring back definition and depth to the ballast.

9. To build up the range of tone in track ballast and to create depth, I applied numerous washes. The effect that a wash has on surfaces such as these is astounding and utterly transformative. The additional bonus when it comes to trackwork is that a wash can easily flow under the rails and

into any small gaps in the track that a brush would otherwise miss.

Washes are also useful in blending together different elements of a build. In this instance, the darker wash blended the rails with the sleepers and obscured any messy or unpainted areas.

10. Several brown, grey and black washes were applied to the ballast to build up a real depth of colour. The edges of the ballast were slightly over-saturated to ensure a good blend between the track and the scenic elements that would be added alongside later.

Work began on the river section, which was made using the tissue roll technique, before several layers of acrylic paint were applied to the surface.

11. As the ballast was left to dry, I turned my attention to other areas of the build. A small area of water had been applied at the bottom of the river bank, which had been created using the toilet roll and PVA technique (see Chapter 4).

After this had been allowed to dry, it was primed and then painted a khaki to begin creating the impression of a 'peaty' river. Washes and additional effects would be added later to build up the depth of colour.

The edges of the track were weathered to hide the polished metal, while the ballast was dry-brushed to add some highlights and extra definition.

12. Once the ballast had dried, the edges of the track were weathered using acrylic paint and a dark drown wash. The acrylic paint created the initial stains of soot and grime, while the wash added depth to the inner corner of the rail and blended in the base with the ballast. The important top face of the rail was constantly wiped to ensure that it was clean for the smooth running of locos.

Although much of the river bank would be covered with grass and foliage, the base was prepared with a mixture of brown paints and washes in case any areas should be left exposed.

13. As the track was again left to dry, the river bank was based in a coat of brown ready for foliage and grass to be added. Several washes were also applied for two reasons. The first was to add greater depth and variety to the earth should any areas be left exposed after adding scenery, and the second was to add a greater blend between the base of the river bank, the small strip of pebble shore and the river itself. The pebble shore had been made using the exact same mix as the ballast.

While the base was left to dry and settle, work began on preparing the scenic materials. Grass was made from paintbrush bristles, which were then stained with acrylic paint. Water was added to help spread the paint evenly through the bristles, but too much would create a sludgy mess.

Extra weathering was added to the trackwork to mimic the build-up of soot and grime over many years of use.

14. Dry-brushing and weathering powders were used to add more tone to the track, ballast and river bank. Due to the passing of both steam and diesel locomotives, soot and grime naturally builds up on the centre of the track in particular, so a very dark brown from an eyeshadow palette was smeared into the centre. A light cream acrylic was dry-brushed on the edges of the ballast, in areas that would have escaped any major weathering. Finally, the river bank, again in areas that could be exposed, was coated in a light eyeshadow colour to create a dry, dusty earth tone.

15. The next stage was to make the foliage and static grass, using a combination of the techniques covered in Part II. The first element to go down on the scene was some grass, which would be right against the track ballast and pebble shore. The bristles of a large DIY brush were cut up into a container before being mixed with a mixture of various colours of acrylic paint and some water. The water helps to saturate the bristles and move the colour around but it does increase the drying time substantially, so think carefully about the amount that you want to add.

Drying times for this technique can be extensive, especially in colder climates; placing the material in a window exposed to sunlight is an efficient way of speeding up the process.

16. The various samples of foliage and grass were left out to bake in the April sun. While the top layer of material may feel dry to the touch, it is important to move the material around to expose the lower layers, which can very easily remain wet for a considerable amount of time. Where possible, place things to dry in a window exposed to strong sunlight; other methods, such as using a heat gun or a hairdryer, can cause much more mess than they are worth.

The finished collection of scenic materials ready to be applied to the diorama. Have everything prepared prior to this step to give greater flexibility in mixing various colours and textures.

17. Once dry, the various flock and scatter were put into containers ready to be applied to the scene. Keeping materials separate is of course essential to ensure consistency, but do not be afraid of mixing some of them in a separate container. It is rare in nature to see individual elements of an environment completely separate from one another, with the most notable example being fallen leaves from a tree scattering over a wide area and mixing with grass and hedges.

A layer of PVA was applied to the river bank before several layers of grass and foliage were arranged on the surface. Diluted PVA was applied once finished to set everything in place. PVA was also applied to the river surface to create a glossy finish.

18. A thin to medium layer of PVA glue was applied to the river bank before both the grass and bushes were added to the scene. This was simply a case of looking at image references and building up a credible density of foliage. Once the arrangement was satisfactory, the same glue mixture that was used to secure the ballast in place was used on both the grass and foliage. A layer of glue had already been applied to the base, but a dousing of the adhesive mixture would soak through the sponge and ensure that all elements of the scene were secure. Finally, a layer of PVA was brushed onto the river and stippled as it dried to finish off the water.

Extra details, such as sticks and branches, were added to create more interest and natural variety.

19. To add a bit more variety to the foliage (as everything was looking a little too neat and unrealistic), I added two more weathering steps. The first was to dry-brush additional colours into the foliage to take away some of the greens, which were a little too vivid, and to make the surface texture a little more uneven. The second step was to cut up some brown brush bristles, which were then very lightly scattered unpainted into the foliage to mimic branches and sticks. After another light coating of watered-down PVA, the scene was left to dry completely.

Summary

While this approach to modelling scenery requires a little more time and patience, the quality of results and financial savings hopefully speak for themselves. With these methods, not only can just the right amount of material be made up on request but a great deal more customisation is possible. Individual bags of scatter in exactly the right shade need not be bought when a cheap set of acrylics can do that job perfectly.

That being said, buying from the shop can be much more efficient – especially when working on a larger layout. However, should you run out just before a baseboard is covered, or if you are making just a small shelf layout, or if you are a wargamer looking to make the tiniest of character stands, then these techniques form a suitably cheaper alternative without compromising on quality.

TIPS

If it is your intention to attempt to replicate a similar scenic diorama, I would advise the following:

- Prepare all your textures and scenic elements in advance, and have as great a variety as possible.
- Account for drying times, which will be extensive when using these techniques.
- Do not underestimate the importance of priming the base before applying the scenic elements. Any white areas left exposed will be a frustrating eyesore.
- Look out for glue pooling and running over the surface. While this can be used to your advantage, it can quickly run out of control and potentially ruin completed areas of the build. Cleaning supplies on stand-by are a must.
- Use your image references. Nature is rarely neat and organised, so try to let go of a designer's eye and allow a little chaos into the build.

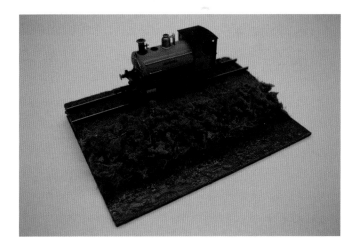

Final scenic build. Although just a short section has been modelled, this could be applied to an entire layout easily. Simply bulk up on materials beforehand.

CONCLUSION

The intention of this book was to open people's minds to the wealth of materials that can be found in our very homes and the amazing range of projects they can be applied to. In pursuit of this aim, we have raided kitchen cupboards, garages, spice racks, supermarkets and more to gather a true menagerie of items. Using the most basic of toolkits, these items have been transformed into many things, from water and grass to brickwork and interior furnishings, exploring the many other directions that could be taken along the way.

It is my sincere hope that, after reading this book, you have gained an insight into not just a whole new range of materials and media but also that you have been inspired to start experimenting and searching for your own techniques. The examples in this book are just a handful that I have learned or have discovered over the years and there are many more out there being developed by the most amazing craftspeople… and, as always, still waiting to be discovered.

GLOSSARY

Adhesive Glue

Bevel When an edge becomes angled or sloped; a common side-effect of sanding

Burr A raised edge that forms when some materials are cut using a scalpel

Doll's house effect A term that refers to the toy-like aesthetic of a model that is generally caused by the use of out-of-scale materials

Dry-brushing The process of using a very small amount of paint on a paint brush to add highlights to a surface – effectively the opposite of applying a wash

Dry fit The process of connecting two components without adhesive, typically used to check that measurements and positioning is correct

Fabrication Another term for making

Finish How the surface of the model will finally be presented. This generally refers to sanding, painting and varnishing

Flock Small particles of soft material, typically sponge; commonly found in railway modelling

Flush When two materials or components sit perfectly with one another at the same level

Ground cover Typically refers to natural scenes and the combination of textures, for example earth, grass, leaves, bushes

Kit bashing The process of building using spare model kit pieces, found objects and materials

Oil-based Solutions that contain oil; they can generally be thinned and washed with mineral spirits

Porous Describes materials that can soak up water

Priming Applying a preliminary layer of paint that improves the bonding of subsequent paint layers to a particular surface

Scatter Small particles of hard material, typically stones; commonly found in railway modelling and wargaming

Scratch building The process of building using raw sheet materials

Sheet material Flat panels of material, for example an A3 sheet of card

Solvent-based Solutions containing ethanol

Washes Ink-like solutions that emphasise shadows and detail; the opposite of dry-brushing

Water-based Solutions that contain water; can generally be thinned and washed with water

Weathering Also known as distressing; the process of aging or degrading the quality of a material or surface texture

Working time The duration of time between mixing two components that react with one another to the subsequent mixture becoming unworkable

INDEX